THE
MARRIAGE
BENEFIT

THE MARRIAGE BENEFIT

The Surprising Rewards of Staying Together

MARK O'CONNELL, PhD

SPRINGBOARD PRESS

NEW YORK   BOSTON

Springboard Press
Hachette Book Group USA
237 Park Avenue, New York, NY 10017
Visit our Web site at www.HachetteBookGroupUSA.com.

Springboard Press is an imprint of Grand Central Publishing. The Springboard name and logo are trademarks of Hachette Book Group USA, Inc.

Printed in the United States of America
First Edition: July 2008

10 9 8 7 6 5 4 3 2 1

Library of Congress Cataloging-in-Publication Data

O'Connell, Mark, 1954–
    The marriage benefit : the surprising rewards of staying together /
Mark O'Connell.—1st ed.
        p. cm.
    Summary: "The Marriage Benefit reveals how staying together in midlife—when it often seems easier to leave—offers big payoffs in mental and physical health and well-being."—Provided by the publisher.
    ISBN-13: 978-0-446-58111-0
    ISBN-10: 0-446-58111-9
    1. Marriage. 2. Commitment (Psychology) I. Title.

HQ734.O28885 2008
646.7′8—dc22   2007043658

Book design by Giorgetta B. McRee

For Alison

CONTENTS

GROWING UP TOGETHER:
MIDLIFE CHALLENGES AND
MIDLIFE RELATIONSHIPS

This is a book about marriage, but it's not the kind of "how to make your marriage better" book that we have come to expect. This is a book about how stretching the boundaries of what we imagine to be possible can turn our intimate relationships into remarkable opportunities for growth and change. This is a book about how our relationships can make *us* better.

And this is also a book that offers a radical and contemporary answer to an age-old question. Why stay married? Because our long-term relationships can, at their best, help us to navigate the maddeningly relentless passage of time. They can teach us how to find purpose and meaning even in the face of life's most immovable limits, making growing older an expanding, rather than a diminishing, experience.

A Date

Philip and Marie slipped into the empty seats, a rarity for rush hour on the Lexington Avenue subway. Usually they met at their uptown apartment, often quite late now that Drew was off at college and Kaetlin spent most evenings with her high school friends. But last night Philip had proposed dinner in the Village at a new restaurant he'd seen reviewed in the *Times.*

Marie had been pleased by her husband's suggestion. Things worked fine between them; Philip was kind and fair, and she didn't doubt they loved each other. But they had talked less and less to each other over the past few years, and when they did it was mostly about the business of their marriage—money, kids, social engagements, and the like.

As the train picked up speed, heading downtown from the Fifty-ninth Street station, Philip glanced at his wife and saw her brief return smile. He wanted to talk to her, he knew he could start a conversation about yesterday's argument with Kaetlin, but he wanted something else, and he couldn't find the opening. In their familiarity with each other she somehow seemed to have grown more unfamiliar to him.

Marie had seen Philip's glance, and she wanted to grab her husband's momentary availability. But by the time she could think of anything to say he had opened his briefcase, extracting one of those manila folders that always seemed to occupy the space between them. She, too, opened her briefcase, though she bypassed the briefs and depositions for the college catalogues: Kaetlin would be heading off next fall.

The subway pulled out of Union Square, heading toward Bleecker. In place of the predictable middle-aged disgorgements of the midtown offices, their car now filled with young people; kids dressed in black, with lots of piercings, and with this the quiet turned to laughter and loud conversation.

A woman in her early twenties caught Philip's attention. She's not exactly beautiful, he thought, noting that he'd gone from being awed by the power women held over him to regarding them with some kind of controlling, clinical evaluation. Still, there was something about this girl: the smoothness of her skin, the litheness of her body. But it's more than her looks, he thought, it's that sex is still her currency. Marie was still beautiful to him, but since the kids had been born she had dressed to be taken seriously, not to be sexy.

Marie noticed Philip's interest in the girl. She always noticed when he looked, and always she wanted to ask: "Will you fantasize about her?" "Do you wish I looked like that?" She didn't really fear the answers to these questions, she just wanted to know. When they were younger they had talked about everything, but somehow, over the years, so much of what they thought about seemed to have become off-limits.

Philip had seen Marie notice his glance. Did she know that his looking at women wasn't really about sex but about something else—a time past that he missed, even a part of himself that he seemed to have lost? He wanted to talk to his wife about these things, but something blocked him, embarrassment maybe, and beneath that a lurking sadness that he needed to turn away from.

Now Marie looked at the young woman. She remembered when she was that lean, twenty-five years and two kids ago. She missed the feeling of being alive in her body, of waking up and swinging her legs out of bed, her feet landing lightly on the floor. What was worse, the thickening of her body seemed to have been accompanied by a thickening of her mind. She watched the girl's eyes dart between her companions, taking as much pleasure in the emerging power of her own young being as in the company of her friends, and she remembered when she had felt ironic and sharp, when she had looked at life from those slightly off-kilter angles. She wanted to tell Philip all of this, but she feared he'd see her as even older and less appealing than he probably already thought she was.

The sign for Spring Street appeared through the train's window, and Philip and Marie rearranged themselves. Standing together, they shared a quick smile as he touched her shoulder, gently ushering her toward the door.

WE ARE GROWING OLDER,
BUT ARE WE GROWING UP?

A generation of baby boomers (those born between 1946 and 1964) has reached midlife. Most of us have made the life-defining choices—jobs, spouses, and even, on a deeper level, outlooks and philosophies—that have become the stuff of our lives. If we have worked hard, been wise in our decisions, and, perhaps more than we would like to admit, been blessed with a bit of plain old good luck, our lives hold many rewards and satisfactions.

We have also, however, become acutely aware of the paths we have not taken, of the costs that accompany even our most rewarding choices. What once felt like life-expanding opportunities now feel, more often than we would like, like life-narrowing obligations. Where previously we thought in terms of what could be, now we are faced with daily reminders of what will probably not be. And where before we imagined an unlimited future, now we ask the questions that come with the awareness that time is finite: What must we concede as being unattainable? What will we look back on as having really mattered? And what will be the most rewarding and meaningful way to spend the precious, and hopefully not insignificant, time that remains?

Over the next twenty to thirty years, we baby boomers will need to answer these questions. They are, however, questions that our generation is uniquely ill-equipped to address. Products of a "we can have it all and if we don't somebody is to blame" culture, we hold tight to our already overextended adolescences. We imagine that all gratifications are possible, that all losses are avoidable, and that all constraints are negotiable. As a result, we experience life's hardships and complexities as unnecessary inconveniences rather than defining, meaning-making aspects of being human.

The result? Perhaps more than any previous generation, we

will struggle with the inevitable reckoning with reality that comes with middle and older age. Bluntly speaking, we risk becoming the first generation to die before it actually grows up.

Fortunately, there is help. Powerful help. In the pages that follow, I will argue that our long-term intimate relationships can help us to grow up, or, to put it another way, they can help us to live fully and creatively even as our private hopes and expectations meet the immutable realities that come with our advancing years. Even better, they can help us with core midlife challenges while bringing us joy, allowing us moments of unexpected laughter and lightness, and helping us to become our best selves.

Of course, things that are this good are rarely easy or free. There is also a hard truth lurking in all this good news. For starters, our mutual relationships, like our individual selves, face a litany of midlife problems:

◈ We are dealing with the loss and disruption of our kids leaving home.

◈ We are embarking on the sometimes oppressive task of tallying our losses and disappointments; in life, in work, and, of course, in marriage.

◈ We are trying, often unsuccessfully, to avoid the seduction of infidelity, a seduction that beckons us not only as an alternative to boredom and disappointment, but also as a balm for our growing sense of diminishment.

◈ We are struggling to reengage with each other after years of focusing on work and children.

◈ We are negotiating the often excruciating hardships of increasing medical and health problems.

✧ We are combating the legion of habits and addictions that we have used to mitigate our anxiety, depression, and boredom.

✧ And we are looking to find each other sexually even as our libido is lowered for both biological and psychological reasons.

And if all this weren't daunting enough, we have to meet these challenges within a society that encourages us to think that our wildest wishes and expectations should be seamlessly transformed into our daily realities. A society that tells us that someone or something is to blame when life delivers us anything short of lasting romance, a stunningly attractive partner, great sex, exceptional kids, impeccable health, and easily resolvable disagreements. We have to come to terms with things as they really are, even as we are increasingly inclined to believe that we should be given a "cheat code" whenever the game of life doesn't go our way.

If we baby boomers are poorly equipped to age well, we are even more poorly equipped to age well together.

JASON AND LESLIE PHILLIPS: "LOVE SHOULDN'T HAVE TO BE THIS HARD."

Throughout these pages I will illustrate my ideas with in-depth stories about long-term relationships. Some of the couples that I describe are taken directly from my practice, though carefully disguised. Some of these couples have read what I've written, making corrections when they felt that I portrayed them inaccurately. Others are more loosely cobbled together, based on composites from years of practice.

As you read these stories, please keep in mind: this is not a book about therapy, rather it is a book about the creative, reparative, and transformative potential of lasting intimacy. Therapy can certainly be a useful catalyst, but when it comes to growth and change, a long-term, trusting relationship is at least therapy's equal. (Current research suggests that it is the *relationship* that is the most important factor in therapeutic outcome.) In these pages therapy is meant only to be a privileged lens, one that allows unique access into the intimate lives of some remarkable people. If you hold on to this perspective you will be halfway to the central take-home message of this book: we have the power to change ourselves, often in surprising and important ways. And we change best when we allow ourselves to be changed by someone to whom we are very close.

Finally, because this is a book about what relationships at their best can be, the stories that I have told portray some of the most creative and resourceful couples that I have known over twenty-five years of practice. Please don't be daunted. If we are willing to do the hard work of building loving and trusting relationships, and if we are then willing to risk leaning back into that love and trust in order to be open and real with each other, we can *all* be changed, even in those places that we feel to be most injured, and, it follows, most immovable.

Now let's introduce the first of the many couples that populate this book. Jason and Leslie Phillips show us something about the problems of growing older, and of growing older together. And they also show us how those very problems can be turned into remarkable opportunities for overcoming, indeed for growing through, the central challenges of middle age.

At first glance, Jason and Leslie seemed a good fit. Both were a bit on the short side, slightly overweight, and, it seemed, possessing of a certain shared softness—in both features and demeanor. Their clothes were high-quality without being obviously fashionable, and I noticed that they had arrived at my home office in a Mercedes.

When I asked how I might help, Jason and Leslie shared a wary glance. He took the lead. "We've been married twenty-three years," he noted, his tone pointedly factual. "We were really in love with each other early on, at least I think we were, it seems so long ago. Then the kids came along, and—well, you know what happens. They're almost grown up now—our daughter is already off at college and our son is going to start next year. There weren't any big fights or anything, it just seems like we drifted apart..."

"No big fights?" Leslie glared at Jason, her voice brimming with anger and hurt. "Aren't we having a pretty big fight now?"

"I was just about to get to that," Jason answered, his factual tone persisting in the face of Leslie's fury. "She's referring to the fact that I've been involved with another woman."

The story was a painfully familiar one. Over the past several months Leslie had become suspicious about the unexplained brightening of Jason's mood, the increased care he took with his appearance, and the way their already minimal sex life had become nonexistent. She turned detective, amassing the evidence from numbers on Jason's cell phone, from romantic cards found on his desk that never came her way, and from unusual charges on his credit card. Her husband, once confronted, confessed. He had become involved with a younger assistant at the advertising office he ran.

My job, during our first few sessions, was to try to limit the damage, and, once things had settled down, to help the couple see what could be salvaged. For starters, this meant pointing out that Jason and Leslie were going about things in all the wrong ways.

He was willing to break off the affair, but not the relationship. "She understands me in a way that Leslie never could," Jason said, though I thought I could see him wince at how clichéd his words sounded.

Leslie threw herself back into the sexual relationship with

Jason, hoping that by giving him excitement reminiscent of their early days together she could save their marriage.

While Jason paid lip service to his responsibility for having had an affair, he blamed Leslie for the marriage's coldness and estrangement, and he didn't understand that he had been equally responsible for letting things become stale.

Leslie, similarly, couldn't see her contribution to their marital troubles. She could be bitingly critical, and over the past several years it had become her habit to retreat into four or five glasses of wine every night.

Both Jason and Leslie had conspired to preside over years of growing estrangement, disappointment, and bitterness. Each partner blamed the other, and neither talked about his or her own responsibility for things.

It took a few sessions to establish some ground rules. First off, did they want to try to repair things? Leslie immediately indicated yes, and when Jason, after a moment's pause, added, "That's why we're here," his conviction surprised me. Well, I noted, there were things each would have to do.

Jason would need to break things off entirely with the woman he had been seeing; as long as he could turn to her whenever things got hard with Leslie, he would be less inclined to commit himself to the kind of work that would be needed.

Leslie would have to stop drinking; alcohol enabled her to retreat from the feelings that she needed to talk about with Jason.

Jason needed to take a hard look at his notion that the problem had to do with the lack of excitement and romance: this belief would lead them away from building the foundation they needed to repair things.

And Leslie needed to stop trying to appease Jason by providing that excitement.

"I suspect that, at least right now, you can trust hard, painful talks more than great sex," I told them. "And you've got to work on how you have those talks. You've got to find a way to replace all this blame and defensiveness with a willingness to be open about how you feel, about what you want, about who you really are."

Jason was skeptical about my plan. "All that sounds like such hard work," he said. "It's not that I can't work hard, I've done it all my life. But I'm tired. Marriage, raising kids, my job. Where's the fun? I don't expect it to be like when we first met, but I need there to be a little more life and understanding."

"Understanding?" Leslie interrupted, her voice dripping with contempt. "Is that why you look at the pictures of celebrities in bikinis while we're waiting in line at the supermarket, why your eyes follow every young thing that walks by you? To feel more understood?"

I considered stepping in here. Leslie had a right to be furious, but we were still trying to establish a framework within which the couple could talk without things spiraling into blame and recrimination. To my surprise, however, Jason softened things with some subdued but heartfelt words. "I *am* having trouble with being just one more middle-aged guy who no woman would ever look twice at," he said. "I can't stand the idea that my life is nothing special, OK? But what exactly is the point of all this hard work? It just seems—I don't know— love shouldn't have to be this hard."

WHY STAY MARRIED?

From Philip and Marie to Jason and Leslie, from basically good relationships struggling with the accumulated weight of compromise that occurs when two selves must find breathing room in a space that often seems to have room for only one, to relationships shredded by acrimony, grievance, hurt, and disappointment, the same advice applies: know yourself. Recognize and respect your differences. Talk to each other. Be respectful. Reinforce the positives and minimize the negatives. Don't blame. Be honest with each other. See things from each other's perspective. Don't judge. As a psychologist who has tried to help many couples with their relationships, I know firsthand that implementing this advice will make a relationship better.

Sounds good, but now let's throw a wrench in the works: Is making our relationships better good enough? For that matter, is even a "good" relationship good enough, particularly now that advances in fertility technology, changing attitudes about single parenthood, shifting moral sensibilities, and other alterations in our social and economic landscape have provided viable alternatives to traditional marriage? What if it is no longer enough to merely make one's relationship "better"?

If marriage is to be anything more than an encumbrance, a vestigial holdover from another time and another convention, we'd best ask a question that we rarely, if ever, ask: *why stay married?* Well, of course we do ask this question, but usually we ask it in the spirit of a rhetorical exercise in which we already assume the answer, or else we ask it in moments of frustration and despair, lamenting the fact that we have to choose between the rock of staying in a lousy marriage and the hard place of divorce. Rarely do we *really* ask ourselves why we stay married. Rarely do we enter into an open-minded exploration with the intent of finding a meaningful, rather than a conventional, reason for all of the sacrifice and commitment required to make an intimate relationship last.

As it turns out, this is a terrific time to ask ourselves why we get, and stay, married. It's a terrific time because for this baby-boom generation, at this life stage and at this moment in cultural time, there is a relevant and contemporary answer. That answer—that our long-term intimate relationships can change us, that they can make us better people—is not, as it might seem on first impression, a self-serving rationalization. It is not just another way of asking "What's in it for me, anyway?" Indeed, the opposite is true: at their best our intimate relationships are life-enhancing crucibles in which we can learn to trade in our at times adolescent self-centeredness for more real and enduring values. These include:

- ❧ **Knowing ourselves:** Being part of a long-lasting relationship is the best way to more deeply know ourselves.

- ❧ **Keeping our memories alive:** Sharing a history with someone we love helps us to remember.

- ❧ **Aging creatively:** An intimate relationship can make the time of growing older one of expanding, rather than diminishing, possibility.

- ❧ **Being more generous:** Our intimate relationships can help us to grow into our best, and least self-centered, selves.

- ❧ **Accepting ourselves:** Lasting intimacy can teach us to appreciate, rather than deny, our human fallibility.

- ❧ **Continued growth:** Intimate partners can help each other to achieve the relentless renegotiation of self that is the hallmark of vitality, change, and growth.

- ❧ **Finding freedom through our limitations:** The most direct path to freedom lies in remaining true to our commitments.

- ❧ **Deeper love:** Love *can* get better over time, and *really* loving someone is the most important thing we do in our lives.

- ❧ **Reaping the rewards of our emotional investment:** There is a mother lode of untapped possibility in the lives that we already have.

Appreciating the degree to which our intimate relationships can bring us these benefits will help all of us.

It will help those of us who are involved in relationships characterized by distance, acrimony, injury, and mistrust. One of the reasons for the low success rate of most marital therapies is that while we know the nuts and bolts of what to do to make things better, we don't know *why* we're doing all that hard work in the first place. Having a sense of purpose will enable us to more easily make sorely needed changes.

It will help those of us who already have good relationships. Without a sense of relevance and purpose even our "good" relationships are but a fraction of what they could be. Understanding that our relationships can be powerful forums for personal growth and real change will make even the best of our relationships better.

And it will help all of us baby boomers; those of us who have good relationships, those of us who have bad relationships, and all of us who fall in between. It will help us because a lasting, loving relationship can enable us to meet the signature challenge of growing older: that of meeting the harder, nonnegotiable edges of reality—of time, of aging, and of loss—with just the right mix of realism, vitality, and hope.

"IT'S NOT PERFECT, BUT IT'S REAL."

Three years after we first met, Jason, Leslie, and I were still speaking weekly. It had been a hard time. One year after we began, Leslie had been diagnosed with ovarian cancer. Her ovaries had been removed, and she had undergone several months of radiation therapy. Metabolic changes related to the menopause that followed had caused a significant weight gain, and she was only recently learning to live with the nagging terror of a recurrence. Yet despite these hardships, or perhaps even in part because of them, both Jason and Leslie had grown.

Leslie was able to hear that she shared responsibility for the couple's troubles. She quit drinking, and she became better at talking with Jason without resorting to the biting negativity behind which she often hid. "I couldn't see what I had," she eventually told us. "I could only see what I didn't have, and I held him responsible for everything that wasn't the way I thought it should be."

Jason, too, had found his way back to the better self that he had lost over the years. Shortly after our meetings began, he had ended his extramarital relationship, and since then he had remained faithful to Leslie. He had been kind and supportive through his wife's illness. He had also gotten himself into individual therapy, which had helped him to see how much his affair had been an effort to counter the feeling that he was "just one more middle-aged guy—who no woman would ever look at twice."

What Jason and Leslie had wasn't magic—they still argued often, they made love infrequently, and there certainly wasn't a whole lot of romance between them. Nevertheless, their arguments were less characterized by blame and recrimination, and more often led to better understanding. That they made love at all was an improvement, and it meant a great deal to both that they had reestablished a life between their bodies. And as for romance, well, as Leslie put it, "Look, we're not exactly a 'hot' couple, but we've learned to take better care of each other. The fact that Jason wanted to touch me at all when I was sick, when I felt less than human—that meant the world to me."

So things were better. Not earth-shatteringly fantastic, but better. As Jason said, "I never thought I could be happy with a relationship like this, but I am. Well, maybe happy is the wrong word. Maybe something more like satisfied, some days even content. It's not perfect, but it's real."

"It's not perfect, but it's real." Here, in a simple phrase, is the essence of what our generation so often fails to grasp. And because we regularly value the seductive gloss of perfection over more substantial, if more limited, real-world satisfactions, we fail to appreciate what we have, and we insulate ourselves from potentially transformative collisions with the world around us.

In the following exchange, you can hear how Jason and Leslie had been able to grow and to mature together. Jason began:

"We went to western Massachusetts this weekend for Susie's graduation (Susie was the daughter who was already attending college just as the therapy began). We were standing there watching all these young people about to head off into their lives. It should have been a happy moment; I'm proud of Susie. But instead I was feeling sorry for myself, like, 'Why can't I have the kind of opportunities those kids have?' I was hating myself too. How come I'm so self-centered, all I can think about is myself when it should be her day?"

Jason took a sip from his bottled water, and then continued: "Then I looked over at Leslie. There were tears in her eyes. When I saw her crying I went from being pissed and it's all about me to being human again. I put my arm around her shoulder, I felt how different her body feels since she was sick. I thought about what it would have felt like if I had been at the graduation alone. You know, it's funny. My memories aren't only mine. They're ours. We made our daughter together. We raised her together. If Leslie wasn't there, it's not just that moment that wouldn't be the same. Even the past would be different."

Leslie gave Jason's forearm a gentle touch of familiarity, and then she turned to me and said: "It was one of those beautiful spring days, the air cool, the sun warming your face just slightly. I was crying because I was happy. I also was thinking about how I almost wasn't there. When Jason put his arm around me I thought about his affair. I was so angry back then, I couldn't forgive him. I'm not excusing what he did—in some ways I'll never get over it—but in another way I understand. I was strangling the life out of him. I couldn't let him want anything, and I couldn't talk to him about what I wanted and needed."

With these words Leslie looked back to Jason. More playfully now, she punched his arm, saying, "If you ever do it again I'll kill you, but you know what? If someone could make it so it never happened, well, I'm not so sure I'd want that."

INTIMATE RESOLUTIONS

By leaving behind their bitterness and grievance, by learning together to tolerate their pains and their losses, Jason and Leslie were able to embrace each other, and their lives, more fully. Three simple and hard-won principles keyed their success.

First, they got very real—with themselves and with each other. They shed their illusions and entitlements, and by forcing themselves to be open and honest about their insecurities and disappointments they let go of the armor that kept them distant from each other.

Second, they instituted playful rituals that served as ongoing reminders of their commitment to each other. Jason made a point of touching Leslie every morning and evening, reminding himself that the changes in her body reflected her brush with death. Leslie sat with Jason every evening, alcohol-free glass of wine in hand, and asked him about his day; this symbolized her decision to stop drinking, and her commitment to be more open and connected. And together they developed a humorous routine in which they bantered about how each had almost left the other—he for a younger woman, she, as he put it, "for God."

And third, they took a series of intimate risks. They gave up anesthetizing habits and distractions like wine and affairs; they made their marriage and the growth of their better selves more important than their own narrowly defined self-interests; and they forced themselves to be more genuine and honest with each other, even about things that were quite painful. They found creative ways to be vulnerable and authentic together, thus making contact in the same deep and private places that they had once fiercely protected.

Being real together, playing together, and taking intimate risks to gether. As you read, please keep these three principles in the forefront of your mind. They will serve as an organizing framework for the backbone of this book, the eight resolutions that will direct and encourage us as we build relationships in which we can change and grow, even, and in many ways especially, as we confront the challenges of middle age and beyond.

Eight "resolutions." In contrast to today's New-Age appropriation of the concept of "intention"[1] (simply declaring our intentions, we are told, will bring us happiness, youth, health, lovers, money, good parking spots, and whatever else strikes our myopic and self-centered fancies),[2] the word "resolution" suggests something a little grittier, a little more commonsensical and down-to-earth. Resolution, defined as "a formal expression of will or intent," conveys the idea that we have to stick our necks out, that we have to *actually do* something, in order to get what we want. Each of the resolutions outlined in this book, it follows, is organized around the conceptualization of an important goal or aspiration, a kind of mental Post-it that, when kept in mind, can point us in the right direction. And each also requires persistent, willful, and goal-directed activity.

Taken together, all eight can be thought of as North Stars, as guiding ideas that we can reach out for throughout our relationships.

Now, armed with this hefty dose of realism, here are the eight decidedly nonmystical resolutions that, when considered together, comprise an action prescription for building better relationships that will, in turn, make us better people.

The first four,

- **Embrace a longer-lasting definition of love**
- **Celebrate your differences**
- **Have real sex**
- **Find freedom through commitment**

I've called "shared necessities."
The second four,

- **Believe in something more important than yourselves**
- **Give up your habits and addictions**
- **Forgive and give thanks**
- **Play**

I've called "shared choices."

Eight intimate resolutions, and one powerful path to a better relationship *and* a better self.

And now one final note of sobriety and caution: little that is truly worthwhile is obtained without risk. The promise of this book—a better relationship leading to a better self—is no exception. These resolutions dare us to approach the very edges of intimacy from which we are most compelled to retreat. They give us permission to delve into our worst selves, always in the hope of growing further into our best selves. And they challenge us to remove the constraints of superficial civility in order to explore those parts of ourselves that we find most foreign and most frightening. They are, in effect, high-risk, high-reward propositions.

Given how adept we seem to be at tearing each other to shreds in our intimate relationships, even when we are trying to keep things safe, these resolutions are serious, and even, under the wrong conditions, dangerous medicine.

Which means that safety is paramount. If these eight resolutions are to be constructive and not destructive, they need to be undertaken from the foundation of a good relationship. Sure, they will themselves make a relationship better—appreciating each other's differences, commitment, and the willingness to forgive are, for example, essential elements of all good relationships—but other basic relationship building blocks that are not the focus of these pages are equally essential to safety. Once again, know yourself; talk to each other; be respectful; reinforce the positives and minimize the negatives; be honest with each other; see things from the other's perspective; don't judge: these and more serve as necessary ground rules for keeping relationships safe.

It takes hard work to make love last. That hard work, however, is worth the effort. From a place of safety, from an atmosphere of caring, kindness, respect, and honesty, we can ask our relationships to be more than merely "good." We can ask them to help us become our best selves.

At its best, middle age is a time of seeking. From injurious adventures like having an affair, to benign but superficial acts like buying a sports car, we try to make our way back to our younger selves. From simple, everyday activities like planting a garden and taking up ballroom dancing, to more adventurous pursuits like traveling and beginning a second career, we fight against the shadows of encroaching time by seeking new growth and new meaning.

This book is based on the belief that the most life-expanding possibilities imaginable can be found in the lives that we already have, and that the mother lode of these possibilities lies in the unexplored depths of our long-term intimate relationships.

The eight resolutions described in these pages will help us to build relationships in which we can find private meaning (even in a culture that often leads us away from that which is most human and most meaningful). They will help us to create relationships in which we can appreciate, rather than deny, our human fallibility. And, particularly relevant to us graying baby boomers, they will help us to forge relationships in which we can make the time of growing older one of expanding, rather than diminishing, possibility.

Our intimate relationships should change us. They should cause us to grow. There is something missing if they don't.

PART ONE

SHARED NECESSITIES

CHAPTER I

EMBRACE A LONGER-LASTING
VISION OF LOVE

This book is organized around two simple principles:

First, if we are to get better as we grow older we will need to find growth and meaning *through* the very hardships and limitations that we often seek to avoid and deny.

Second, more than any other means available to us, our long-term intimate relationships can help us with this critical life task. By opening ourselves to intimately knowing, and intimately being known by, someone different and separate from ourselves, we can uncover the world of untapped possibility that lies unexplored within our own selves.

By now it is probably obvious that we're not talking about a quick fix. If our relationships are to be all that they can be, if they are to become opportunities for meaningful change and growth, we will need to give them time. And in this age of fast and easy gratification giving things time is becoming a lost art.

This is particularly true when it comes to love.

Kurt and Felicia, a haggard-looking couple who appeared to be in their early forties, arrived at my office after eight years of marriage, two children, countless fights, and, more recently, months of numbed indifference to each other. "We both think it's pretty much over," Felicia said, by way of introduction, "but we decided we owe it to the kids to give it one last try." I found sitting with Kurt and Felicia quite unnerving; they rarely looked at each other, they never touched, and they rarely smiled. I felt like I imagine an oncologist feels on meeting a patient who has neglected a malignancy for too long: I suspected that I could do little but ease the couple's pain as their marriage died.

Still, we tried. Initially Kurt and Felicia's relationship had been quite passionate. "We spent the first year in bed together," Kurt said. "But as time went on we started fighting. Then we thought maybe having kids would help, but, no surprise, that didn't work. Now it's like our relationship isn't even important enough to fight about. What's so hard to understand, though, is that we were so into each other early on. Doesn't that mean we loved each other? Shouldn't there still be something there?"

For six months I tried to help Kurt and Felicia find out whether something was still there. Each session they would recount their efforts to recapture their early passion. I would suggest, at first gently, and over time more firmly, that these efforts weren't going to get them very far; they needed to accept the fact that their relationship had changed, and they needed to get to know one another in a more intimate and honest way. Each session they would dutifully concur, but they would return the next week to tell me about how their latest attempt to rekindle romance had flopped. Whether it was that they'd tried a romantic weekend but had argued, or that they'd tried Tantric sex but had gotten bored, they couldn't seem to move away from the notion that the solution lay in returning to the beginning. Finally they decided to stop trying. "We're not angry at each other," Felicia said. "We just don't love each other anymore. We're going to call it quits."

And so they did.

In the beginning of a relationship it's pretty easy to say what love is. As the fairy tales and love stories tell us, love begins with the shiny, exhilarating, heart-pounding experience of romance and passion. As Dr. Luce, the fictional expert on human sexuality in Jeffrey Eugenides' *Middlesex*, puts it, falling in love is a "drugged and happy time where you sniff your lover like a scented poppy for hours running."[1]

But then, as Kurt, Felicia, and the rest of us have learned, comes the well-known rub. The intoxicating timelessness of early passion does, inevitably and without fail, end, and with this the real-world living begins. Can this post-romance time also be called love? Is struggling with conflict, difference, and disillusionment part of love, or is it only love when we are sniffing each other like scented poppies?

In this chapter, I will argue that love is a long-lasting phenomenon that changes and evolves across our life spans. Assuming this mind-set won't be easy: these days the addictive, heightened excitement of falling in love is a better fit for our feel-good culture than are the more tempered rewards that can come from loving over the long haul. But doing so will be worth the effort: by expanding our understanding of what love can be, we will improve our relationships, and our lives, in surprising and powerful ways.

Embrace a longer-lasting vision of love. This is the first of eight intimate resolutions we'll examine in these pages. By rejecting the self-help snake oil sold by the most egregious of the marriage books, the ones that promise to "bring never-ending passion to your relationship," we will arm ourselves with the understanding that the time that follows romance is not an unfortunate, if necessary, compromise, but an opportunity for real and enduring growth and change. And by expanding our vision of love beyond the heightened but transient excitement of early passion, we will give ourselves what Kurt and Felicia were missing: a reason to accompany each other through the daunting but potentially life-enhancing challenges of growing older.

MICHAEL AND SUSAN SMITHSON:
MAKING LOVE LAST

"I can't even begin to tell you how much I don't want to be here," Michael Smithson began. "We've been married thirty years—by the way, how old *are* you? You look like you could almost be one of our kids." Michael's tone was more playful than challenging, and I answered with a simple smile.

Michael smiled back, and then continued, his voice softening. "Anyway, like I said, we've been married thirty years, and we have a good relationship. But something has come up that we're having trouble dealing with." Michael turned to his wife, and then, with a sly wink, added: "Or maybe I should say something hasn't come up."

"You are *so* bad," Susan interjected, waving her husband away in mock disgust. Then, turning toward me, she said: "But this is already good. I think that's the first time he's made a joke about it since the surgery."

Michael and Susan appeared to be in their early sixties. He was trim and wiry, with thinning hair that was neatly gelled into place, and piercing brown eyes. He had dressed casually in jeans and a sport shirt. She seemed more elegant. Her gray hair was tied back in a bun, and she had dressed in a skirt, blouse, and tastefully matching scarf.

Michael took the lead in telling their story. "Two years ago I had surgery for prostate cancer, and even though my surgeon— who by the way is at the top of my hit list—told me he could do a nerve-sparing operation, I haven't been able to get an erection since. I know I'm not supposed to feel this, but I don't feel like much of a man." Michael, who had been leaning forward, now sat back in his chair, relaxed a bit, and turned to Susan with a relieved smile that seemed to say: "There, I said it."

Michael's sense of masculinity wasn't the only casualty of the surgery. Susan, too, was suffering: "The doctors say that there isn't much chance that the cancer has spread," she said. "I tell myself that's what really matters. But it's hard for me too. I know this isn't exactly politically correct, but I felt like more of a woman when I could have him inside me."

Over the past two years Michael and Susan had devoted themselves to reviving their sexual life. They'd tried Viagra, but despite the surgeon's reassurances Michael had suffered extensive nerve damage, and the medicine wasn't effective. They had tried sex therapy, but, as Michael put it, "The problem is with the plumbing, not the technique." They had even tried acupuncture, but that hadn't worked. What had once come easily now felt like hard work. Even worse, they avoided anything remotely erotic—kissing, snuggling, and even hugging—because merely touching each other reminded them of what they had lost.

"I'm thinking of having another surgery," Michael said. "My urologist said he could put an inflatable tube in the shaft of my penis, and I could have erections by pumping some device embedded beneath my skin. The guy told me: 'All you have to do is pump yourself up.' He sounded like one of those guys on *Saturday Night Live*, what were their names? Hans and Franz? '*Vee are going to pump you up!*' Michael paused, and then added softly: "But I don't want a balloon in my dick, so I guess I have—we have—a decision to make."

OVERCOMING AN EARLIER CHALLENGE

Time and time again, both in our individual lives and in our intimate relationships, we face the same core dilemmas. They reemerge with each life phase, always in slightly altered guise. Each time we solve them, usually by way of partial and temporary solutions, we grow and develop. We are all, in a sense, the sum of our imperfect solutions.

Michael's parents had worked blue-collar jobs until retiring with small pensions. He had two younger brothers and two younger sisters, none of whom had finished college. Michael, in contrast, had worked his way through college and law school, and when he first met Susan he was a hard-charging guy two years short of making partner at his law firm. Beneath his meteoric success, however, he was also an insecure young man who felt he had a lot to prove.

Susan, on the other hand, was a child of privilege. Her mother and father had both come from generations of wealth, and their sole form of work involved managing the family trust. She had attended the best schools, and when she met Michael she was teaching at a private elementary school for a salary that she didn't need.

Early on these differences in background made for a good fit. Susan's interest in Michael served as an antidote for his simmering insecurity: "I remember the first time I brought her home all my old buddies were totally tongue-tied. The idea that a woman like her would be interested in me meant that I had made it."

Michael's rough-hewn competitiveness and disdain for those who didn't work hard, meanwhile, fit neatly with a kind of reverse snobbery that Susan had developed. In one of our first sessions she told the following story: "Just after I met Michael I went hiking in the White Mountains with some friends. The trail ended at this campsite, and all these families were there with their trailers and their tents. The air was full of barbecue smoke and the sound of kids playing, and I thought about how my parents, with their fancy country-club parties, would never be caught dead doing something like that. But it seemed to me that those kids were the luckiest kids in the world. I know this sounds condescending, but Michael reminded me of that world."

Michael and Susan complemented each other in many of their most vulnerable and uncertain places, and during the first several months of their relationship they did each other a world of good. Far more than his success in college, law school, and work, Susan's desire for Michael made him feel like he had made it as a man. Susan, meanwhile, found similar benefit in Michael's attraction to her. "My mother is the real-life version of that frigid WASP that Mary Tyler Moore played in *Ordinary People*. She has no sense of herself as a woman, and she never made me feel the least bit feminine either. I could feel how much Michael wanted me. When we got together I replaced this cold, tight picture I had of myself with something more womanly and alive."

As was the case for Jack and Felicia, Michael and Susan's relationship began with a powerful early chemistry. But alas, as was the case for Jack and Felicia, indeed as is the case for all of us, the intoxicating timelessness of early passion did end. What was more, as is also often the case, when this end came the same differences that catalyzed the couple's early chemistry were precisely those that began to chafe. The trouble first appeared over money. Even though Michael was becoming a successful lawyer, Susan's trust fund earned the couple far more each year than did Michael. This apparent piece of good fortune touched on Michael's still-present feelings of insecurity, and he began to prop himself up by demeaning his wife. Susan, in turn, felt hurt by Michael's criticisms, and, taking a page out of her mother's book, she retreated into a state of cold aloofness.

A few years passed and two children arrived, a boy and a girl. By this time Michael was working virtually nonstop during the week, and on weekends he often returned to his old neighborhood to hang out at the bar with his childhood friends. Susan left her teaching job, and she began to take the children to her parents' country club, spending afternoons watching them swim in the pool while she and her mother drank wine and gossiped. The distance increased even further, as did a spiral of hurt and hurting, and eventually Michael and Susan found themselves looking at one another across an uneasy divide.

Where Kurt and Felicia failed, however, Michael and Susan succeeded.

Perhaps ten years after Michael and Susan had married, Michael's father died of cirrhosis. "I remember his funeral," Michael told us, his voice turning wistful as he remembered back twenty years. "I was sitting next to my mother in the front row of the church, and all that I could remember were those Saturday nights when my mother would send me down to the bar to tell him to come home. Then all of a sudden it hit me that the only reason my family looked any different from the family that I grew up in was that we had money. Deep down, things weren't different at all."

After his father's death, Michael resolved to change. He stopped hanging out in his old neighborhood, and he began to spend more time with his family. Susan was deeply moved. "That was a real turning point in our relationship," she noted. "My father gave us these big presents, but he had so much money it never really meant anything. That Michael was willing to make sacrifices for our family meant the world to me. And it made me do my own reality check. One of the reasons my father spent his life at the country-club bar was that my mother was so cold to him. I had to ask myself—was I any different?"

"We never got our relationship back to those first few months when we were so in love," Susan continued, "but that wasn't the point. And we really haven't had any major troubles since, at least not until now."

That, essentially, was Michael and Susan's story. Over the years the couple had had their share of squabbles and disagreements, but overall their relationship had been a good one. Their children had both graduated from college, and their older son had married. Michael still worked full-time as a senior partner at his law firm, while Susan, who had returned to work, had recently retired from teaching. The couple continued to benefit from Susan's money, but Michael's success, and the strength of their relationship, had made the presence of that wealth feel less onerous over the years. Thus far theirs had been a good life.

Now, however, they faced another challenge: they had to come to terms with the consequences of Michael's cancer.

BIOLOGY'S PROGRAM FOR LONGER-LASTING LOVE

Michael and Susan's relationship had been anything but a compromise. By the time they came to talk with me, they considered themselves best friends, they felt a deep sense of gratitude for their shared lives, and over time each had come to know his or her self through the reliable, sustained reflection of the other. These benefits, which are the sort that can make a world of difference in the quality of our lives, can come to all of us. But they can only do so when our relationships are able to grow and evolve over many years.

Embrace a longer-lasting vision of love: by committing ourselves to this resolution we will not only make our relationships better, we will build relationships that help us to change, to grow, and to grow older with courage, purpose, and conviction.

To pursue this resolution, however, we will have to go against the grain of today's "everything-is-possible-now" culture. We will have to choose deeper but slower satisfactions over the intoxicating and addictive experiences of passion and romance.

We may find some support for our iconoclasm if we understand that by choosing this path we are being true to our brains and our bodies: as it turns out, we are endowed with an embedded biological code that allows, even encourages, love to unfold and grow over the course of our life spans.

Let's take a look at this code, beginning with what happens when we first fall in love.

An elegant bit of physiological software shapes the early days of romantic passion. This software governs two separate but related systems: desire and attraction. Makes sense, given that successful evolution depends on our having both the drive to procreate as well as the ability to focus that drive in the direction of someone who has good genes.

On the drive side of things we're largely talking about testosterone, or, as biologist Helen Fisher calls it, "the hormone of desire."[2] For both men and women, the more testosterone one has the more sexual desire one feels, the more sexual thoughts and fantasies one has, and the more sexual activity one engages in.[3] If we were asked to choose one aspect of our physiologies most likely to be related to early passion, testosterone would get a lot of votes, and indeed women who are in the early stages of love do exhibit increased levels of testosterone.

Of course things are rarely straightforward when it comes to the relationship between minds and bodies.[4] While women in love do demonstrate increased levels of testosterone,[5] men who have recently fallen in love, somewhat surprisingly, evidence decreased levels of the hormone.[6] Why might this be?

Because there's more to falling in love than sex, a fact that takes us from the drive side of the early love equation to the attraction side. Consider an experiment in which subjects who had recently fallen in love underwent brain scans while being shown photographs of their beloveds.[7, 8] These scans were compared to those of subjects who were scanned while watching pornographic videos. The brains of the in-love subjects showed significantly more activity in their reward and pleasure centers. Not surprisingly, these areas are associated with feelings of exhilaration, increased energy, hyperactivity, sleeplessness, ecstasy, loss of appetite, addiction, a pounding heart, and accelerated breathing—all traits associated with being passionately in love.[9]

No surprises yet in this admittedly cursory examination of the biology of love: the days of early romance and passion are governed by potent changes in our physiologies. It's even the case that the brain pathways that govern our falling in love appear to be the same as those that are involved in obsessive-compulsive disorder and addiction.[10, 11] It seems to be the *literal* truth that when we fall in love we become "lovesick," or, to borrow from the musician Robert Palmer, "addicted to love."[12] To quote Mr. Palmer's views on the subject: "You can't sleep, you can't eat... You're gonna have to face it, you're addicted to love."

If we stopped here we might buy into the vision of intimacy articulated by the singer Meat Loaf in his anthem for unhappily married baby boomers, "Paradise by the Dashboard Light." The song's protagonist, desperate to convince his girlfriend to have sex with him, finally gives in to her demand that he promise to "love her to the end of time." Alas, things don't work out so well, and by the song's end we find him praying for that "end of time to hurry up and arrive."

Certainly Meat Loaf's perspective[13] is a familiar one: we have long believed that early passion inevitably gives way to disappointment, boredom, and acrimony. But the fact is, if love really is destined to turn sour after the thrill is gone, it's not the fault of biology. In fact, the opposite is true. Love, according to the vision put forward by science, is not a fleeting, transient experience, one more easily captured and preserved by poets than by real-life couples. Rather it involves complementary and sequential processes that can last a lifetime.[14]

Recently scientists at University College in London gave MRIs to subjects who had been in relationships that had lasted slightly beyond the early months of romance and passion (the couples studied had been together an average of 2.3 years).[15] As with earlier studies of subjects who were in love, they found increased activity in the brain's reward centers. But they also found something else: increased activity in areas that regulate emotion, attention, and working memory.[16] Biologist Helen Fisher postulates that somewhere in between the first half-year and the first two years of a relationship, the brain may begin to lay down and consolidate the kind of cognitive and emotional experience necessary for longer-term attachment.

And then there is that ubiquitous and influential hormone mentioned earlier: testosterone.

Testosterone, it turns out, shapes more than just lust. When men are teenagers testosterone levels are at their highest, and then as men age these levels drop.[17] It follows that as men grow older, and as their relationships move forward in time, biology favors attachment over ardor. What's more, local variations in testosterone levels occur over the course of our life spans. When marriages become less stable testosterone levels rise. Same for when men divorce. On the other hand, when marriages are more stable testosterone levels decrease, as they do, interestingly enough, when men become fathers and when they hold a baby. It appears that testosterone levels shift in response to circumstance in order to support the kind of tempered, enduring relatedness that is conducive to longer-term intimacy and to family life.

Finally there is the matter of oxytocin and vasopressin, or, as Fisher calls them, the "cuddle chemicals."[18] If testosterone is the chemical of desire, then oxytocin and vasopressin appear to be the hormones of long-term attachment.[19] Human mothers secrete oxytocin when they give birth, thus facilitating bonding with their newborns.[20] Furthermore, oxytocin and vasopressin (both of which generate a pleasurable sense of well-being) are associated with trust: when we believe that we are trusted, our brains release oxytocin, and the more oxytocin our brains release the more trustworthy we become.[21] Finally, oxytocin is released by women during intercourse, while vasopressin is secreted by men.[22] These hormones generate a postcoital sense of security and contentment, one that is more moderate, more socializing, and, importantly, more enduring than the heated but fleeting excitement of sexual passion.

In sum, these "cuddle chemicals" appear to serve as renewable glue for the bonding and attachment that are the cornerstones of long-term intimacy.[23]

We are who we are because of an infinitely complex confluence of biology, evolution, culture, and psychology, and love may be the most complex, most impenetrable, and most ineffable of all human experiences. Nevertheless, the biology of human relationships over time holds a message of great importance when it comes to love: love evolves.[24] Long-term attachment is as much a part of the overall puzzle of love as those relatively fleeting, addictive experiences of early lust and attraction.

Now let's leave the laboratory and return to real life. Let's see how staying in love helped Michael and Susan to grow in ways that neither had imagined possible.

DANCING AN OLD DANCE

On several occasions—not only around that difficult time when their children were young but at several other points in their relationship—Michael and Susan had trusted in the same core strengths: they both had highly developed capacities for being honest about their own shortcomings, for accepting and then tackling the specific challenges brought on by different life phases, and, perhaps above all, for regaining their bearings when they began to veer away from their core values and beliefs. Now they leaned on these strengths once again, as they struggled with the difficult decision as to whether or not Michael would have the penile implant surgery.

We began by identifying an old pattern. Michael's impotence had caused an upsurge in his feelings of inadequacy, and he was managing his insecurity in a familiar and problematic way: he had broken out the old jokes about Susan's wealth. She didn't find his references to her work having been "just a hobby" or to her having been a "country-club debutante" particularly funny, but in her sensitivity to Michael's illness she had been slow to call him on his jabs. He criticized and she withdrew: Michael and Susan had danced this dance before, and once they became aware that they had settled into an old and fruitless pattern Michael stopped his teasing, and Susan became more available.

Then Michael and Susan took the next step: they used the reservoir of trust and understanding that they had accrued over the years to talk about whether or not to go forward with the surgery. This meant sorting through what sex really meant to them. As Susan put it: "Why, exactly, would we have the operation? Is it only so that Michael can come inside me? If that's really what we're after, fine, but sex is a pretty complicated thing. It seems to me that before we decide what to do we have to figure out what it is we really want."

Sex in long-term intimate relationships is indeed complicated. Michael and Susan did miss being able to have intercourse, but it was more than the sex itself that they missed. "There's more to sex than sex," said Susan, smiling a wry smile. "I miss having Michael inside me, but more than that, sex has always been a way that we've expressed ourselves. A way that we've been able to feel ourselves through each other. *That's* what I want to have back."

The notion that sex involved mutual self-expression and trust seemed hopeful. The purely physical side of Michael and Susan's sex life would never be the same, but their minds had the potential for a great deal of flexibility. If the problem and the solution lay as much in the mental realm as the physical, there was a good chance that things could get quite a bit better.

So we went to work on the mental side of things. In the first session Michael and Susan had spoken of how anything even remotely erotic reminded them of the cancer, the surgery, and the loss of their sexual relationship. Now, some three months into our work, we began to focus on the trouble they had living with this awareness. Michael explained:

"Lately I've been trying to be physically closer to Susan, but when I get in bed, roll over to her, and put my hand on her breast like I used to do just about every night, all I can think about is that nothing is happening down there. I just want to roll away because of how much I miss what I used to feel, and because I feel like such a failure. I know you're going to say I'm *not* a failure, and Susan tells me the same thing. On one level I know that's true, but hey, I'm a guy, my brain is only my second most important organ."

To use the familiar language of the marriage manuals, Michael and Susan "worked hard" at learning to deal with their pain. Anticipating an important theme, I believe that it would be more true to say that they "played" hard at making a shared place for their most vulnerable and authentic selves.

Over the next several months Michael and Susan committed themselves to touching each other, even though this often caused them pain. They began to develop connected and playful ways to make love that did not involve intercourse. And they learned how to talk, to laugh, to cry with each other through the fear and sorrow that accompanied every moment of physical closeness and pleasure. In these ways they not only found their way back into each other's arms, they found their way back into each other's minds.

"I can still have an orgasm even without having an erection," Michael noted. "It feels good, not as good as it used to, but still good, especially if I don't obsess about how it isn't what it used to be. Same with Susan, sex can still feel really good to her too, but we have to make sure that we stay in touch with each other. You know what else? It feels a little scary to be so open to each other, but it's also kind of exciting. We've gotten a lot more creative about what we do with each other. And no, the specifics are none of your business. Like I told you in that first meeting, you look pretty young to me, and I wouldn't want to shock you."

TOWARD A NEW DEFINITION OF LOVE

Certainly Michael and Susan's decision to pass on the implant surgery would not have been right for everyone. They, however, decided that restoring their ability to have intercourse by mechanical means wouldn't have been right for them. "He had cancer, he had the surgery, he got better, and there are some scars," Susan said. "Like the saying goes, 'It is what it is.' I can accept all that, as long as we can find ways to be together that feel personal and real."

Michael and Susan built their sexual relationship into one that helped them to live creatively with a difficult truth. That truth went beyond Michael's cancer; Michael and Susan were *both* encountering the bodily changes that come with getting older. These changes included not only the physical and psychological assault of serious illness (one in seven men between the ages of sixty and seventy-nine develops prostate cancer,[25] while one in fourteen women develops breast cancer by age seventy); they also included the simple, everyday changes that take place in all of us as our bodies age. These changes are hard in themselves, and they are made all the harder because they cause us to feel inadequate in comparison to today's unrealistic, airbrushed vision of physical health and attractiveness.

Michael and Susan's playful, loving interplay, however, helped them to remain alive and vital even as they faced these later-life challenges. By finding ways to be sexual and real with each other they were able not only to tolerate the ravages of illness and the diminishments of aging, they were able, as they had at numerous preceding life stages, to grow through adversity.

Love is obviously shaped by many forces. In addition to biology, our psychologies, our culture, and the unique dynamics of each relationship come into play. My point in this chapter is not that biology is the only, or even the most important, force behind the intricacies of human love and intimacy. My point is that the biology of love offers us a user-friendly template for understanding that love *does* last beyond those early months when euphoria-inducing chemicals are being released into the pleasure and addiction centers of our brains. The fact is, love can and does last and evolve *across our life spans*.

This understanding gives us two gifts:

First, we grow merely by making love last. One reason that the early days of passion and romance are a source of such unbridled joy is that they are perhaps the only phase of adulthood in which it is healthy to live largely in the pleasure of our illusions. At the same time, our ability to evolve out of this phase into a relationship in which we get to know each other as we *really* are can bring us equally valuable, if more sober, gratifications. A long-term intimate relationship is perhaps the ultimate classroom for learning how to find meaning and satisfaction in a world that is, ultimately and much to our consternation, not going to yield to our omnipotence.

Second, by making love last, by remaining in real and intimate contact with one another over the long haul, we create a space in which several growth-promoting processes can take place. These processes, which I have endeavored to capture through the resolutions spelled out in this book, all require the safety and intensity of a long-term relationship.

Some of the nuts and bolts of creating and sustaining a longer-lasting vision of love are:

- **Create a hopeful, even ambitious vision of what your relationship can be over time.** And then try to live toward that image.
- **Remind each other of the value of your accumulated years.** Appreciate all that you have built, and make certain that your partner knows that you appreciate his or her contribution to those accomplishments. Recognize what you have. Talk about it together. Thank each other for it.
- *Don't* **try to rekindle early passion**. The pleasure of romantic love can, in moments, be recaptured, but the harder you try to get back to the beginning, the less likely you are to be successful (a simple truth that the "bring back your passion" marriage books just don't get). Consider those moments when you are transported back to that earlier time an unexpected gift.
- *Do* **try to hold on to your beginnings by remembering together, and, more formally, by observing the ritual of anniversaries and other important dates.** Remembering the past is not the same as trying to relive it; remembering the past is essential for living fully in the present, and on into the future.
- Above all, **reject the societal message that we are all entitled to perfect bodies, great sex, and endless romance.** This "we can have it all without paying a price" mind-set can cause us to feel that the greater part of our lives together is a booby prize, an unfortunate compromise that comes after the "real" love of early romance. And it causes us to overlook the more grounded, more substantive rewards that come with staying together over time.

Perhaps many readers are now saying, "These suggestions are all well and good, but they assume that my husband/wife and I are already on the same page about this stuff. If that were the case the battle would be more than half won. How do I get him/her to sign on?"

This is an important question. The fact is, it is more the norm than the exception that one member of a couple must take the emotional lead. We tend to assume that this means an emotionally aware woman leading a less emotionally mature man by the nose, but I have learned to be wary of this stereotype. Indeed, in my experience there is much more equality in these matters than is generally assumed.

So what can you do to get your reluctant partner to sign on?

- For starters, **think positively**. If it is up to you to take the lead, consider the apparent inequity an opportunity for your own growth.
- **Speak positively to your partner**. "There is a lot of good that can come from knowing each other for so long" and "I think that there is still a lot that we can learn from each other" can go a long way. "You're so emotionally dim that you only think it's love when you're screwing three times a day" is less likely to be helpful.
- **Lead by example**. This is true for each of the eight resolutions. Your most powerful means of changing your partner is to first change yourself, and then to ask, often implicitly, that your partner join you. So hold on to your own longer-lasting vision of love, believe in it resolutely, and model it for your partner.
- Finally, **trust in the power of time**. Persevere when you get frustrated. Meaningful changes are slow and hard-earned. Be willing to go out on a limb with your beliefs, and, equally important, be willing to stay out on that limb for a long time.

Robert Solomon wisely notes: "We define love in such a way that it could only be a transient experience, and then we wonder—sometimes bitterly—why love doesn't last."²⁶ Well, here's this chapter's take-home message: *we need a new definition of love*.

We need a definition of love that serves as an antidote to our modern belief that life is as it should be only when feel-good chemicals are coursing through the pleasure centers of our brains. We need a definition of love that embraces romance and passion (indeed one would have to be a real curmudgeon to begrudge these wonderful experiences), yet still encourages us to appreciate the way in which love can help us to evolve and grow, through the early months of romance, through more tempered attachment, through building a life together, through aging, and, inevitably, through loss—through all of the seasons of a married life. We need a definition of love that doesn't encourage us to devote our relationships to the single-minded pursuit of keeping romance alive, because the more actively we pursue passion the more elusive it becomes.

And we need, above all, a definition of love that can help us to live and love *with*, rather than *against*, the natural course of time and human nature.

First Weekend

An early September morning on the coast of Maine. There was a touch of cool in the air, noticeably more so than the day before. Jessica smelled a hint of smoke, maybe from a distant woodstove, and the light was just a little more angled, a little less direct, than it had been. It was her favorite kind of day.

She and David were marking their twentieth anniversary. The idea was his; in a surprisingly romantic move, he had suggested a reprise of their first weekend getaway. And he had been talking about that weekend since they arrived, about the wonderful and idyllic time he recalled. Strange, she thought, but her memories were very different from his. For her the weekend was more complicated.

" 'Complicated'? How come whenever I think things are good

you think they're 'complicated'?" David had teased. But that was how she remembered it.

Sure, Jessica also remembered the feelings that her husband had been talking about. They had been together for five months— the happiest five months of her life, she had giddily told her best friend just before they had left. "He's sensitive but he's still a guy," she had said. "Knock on wood, but I think this just might be it." She remembered how startled she had been to hear her own words. Relieved, too. She had begun to fear that she wouldn't be swept into marriage by love, rather she, like her own parents, would have to settle for the best available option.

But the weekend hadn't gone as she'd expected. The trouble had started Sunday morning, a few hours before heading home. They had gotten up early to run on the beach, but instead of going stride for stride like they usually did their paces had been at odds. David had kept edging ahead, telling her she could run faster. On the surface it seemed complimentary, this "you're faster than you think" stuff that guys liked to do, but, as it had with other guys, it felt more controlling than encouraging. "Go on ahead," she had said, "I'll meet you back at the inn." That really would have been okay with her, but he didn't seem to want that, and after the run she had felt a tension that she had not felt with him before.

Later, walking into town for breakfast, there had been an uneasy silence. This was new too; usually the talk just bubbled from both of them. She had taken his hand, but she couldn't seem to find that comfortable place that she had always been able to find. At the restaurant the sense that they had a special secret was missing, that "I bet those people don't know what we were doing with each other an hour ago" feeling that made it so much fun to be out in public.

Now they were sitting across from one another in that very same breakfast place that they had sat in twenty years previously—two almost fifty-year-olds whose children were finally old enough to let them be alone. Jessica had enjoyed the weekend; she had enjoyed coming back here, and she had liked having time alone with David. But she also felt distant from him. She wanted them to remember the weekend together, but his memories were so different from hers that reminiscing left her feeling at odds with him.

She decided to try again.

"You know what my favorite moment of that weekend was?" she asked.

"The fifth time we had sex?" David answered. She knew that he was trying to be playful, but it felt as if he were trying to force her memories into his, and she sensed herself pushing back from him, wanting to hold on to her own mind.

"No." Her voice was gentle but resolved. "The drive home."

"What, you were happy to get away from me?" David was still kidding, but she could tell that he was starting to feel hurt that she didn't remember the same romantic getaway that he did.

"Not at all." Her voice was still serious, but she short-circuited her husband's hurt by taking his hand, and by looking directly into his eyes. "It *was* a complicated weekend, David. But for me that wasn't a bad thing. We were starting to get to know each other. To *really* get to know each other. It was the first time we had to deal with some of the same stuff we've had to deal with over the past twenty years. What I remember is that when we were driving home I tried to talk to you about it, and you didn't get defensive. I still remember what you said: 'Maybe it can't always be like the movies. Maybe we have to get through the harder times too.'"

"I do remember that," David answered softly, returning her gaze. Jessica felt herself relax. All weekend David had wanted to make love, and she hadn't quite been into it. Now she felt herself open to him. "I'll always remember that moment," she continued. "I remember when you dropped me off at my place that night I felt kind of sad, like I'd lost something, but I felt good, too. A different kind of good. That was when I trusted that it was going to work."

CHAPTER II

CELEBRATE YOUR DIFFERENCES

Fetch me that flower; the herb I shew'd thee once:
The juice of it on sleeping eye-lids laid
Will make or man or woman madly dote
Upon the next live creature that it sees,

William Shakespeare
A Midsummer Night's Dream

In William Shakespeare's *A Midsummer Night's Dream*, a magic potion, juice from the "love-in-idleness" flower, causes an unsuspecting recipient to fall madly in love with the first living creature that walks by. This mischievous plant serves as an apt metaphor for one of the defining features of that felicitous bit of chemistry that we call romance: our shiny new lovers may be dearly special to us, but that doesn't mean that we are very good at seeing them for who they really are.

As the heady excitement of early love begins to fade, however, we begin to perceive our highly human, and therefore highly imperfect, partners more clearly. We call this process disillusionment, and we consider it to be the make-or-break moment in lovers' journey through time: if we get through this rocky passageway, the common wisdom has it, we will emerge into a more tempered, more reliable, but certainly less exciting quality of relatedness.

Isn't it odd that we think in such unimaginative and sadly deflating terms about getting to know someone whom we love?

Fortunately the process of disillusionment, of literally shedding one's illusions so as to better know the truth of things, does not have to be one of depressing compromise. In fact the opposite can be true.

Celebrate your differences. This is the second resolution described in this book. When we understand, and then appreciate, our differences—and by "differences" we're not talking about Mars and Venus, about he likes football and she likes dance, or about any other of the infinite surface ways in which we differ from our partners, we're talking about the underlying *fact* that we are different people—we come to know each other more deeply and more honestly. And by doing so we not only build better relationships, we also build better selves.

NOAH AND DEVON ROSENBAUM

Noah and Devon Rosenbaum, mid-forties parents of two children, had been married for fifteen years when they first came to talk with me. Noah, a pediatrician, was short and stocky, with a bushy mustache, a casual but hip style of dress, and dark brown eyes. Devon, a lawyer, was stylishly thin. Her clothing was simple and neat, and her blond hair and blue eyes bespoke her Protestant background.

At first glance Noah seemed to have drawn the short end of the marital stick. He was smart, warm, and apparently insightful, he was generous with gifts, and he frequently told Devon how much he loved her. She was more guarded. She rarely told Noah that she loved him, and not only was she less generous with her gift-giving, she also felt uncomfortable when Noah gave to her. Noah seemed remarkably gracious about this apparently lopsided arrangement, while Devon was quick to suggest that her husband was almost saint-like in his willingness to put up with her. "I'm pretty much just a cold WASP bitch," she told me early on. "I don't know how he stands it."

As is often the case, however, the couple's surface arrangements were as misleading as they were explanatory. After a few months of talking together Noah's tolerance began to give way to irritation, and Devon, who had become less willing to blame herself for everything that went wrong in the relationship, began to talk about what wasn't working so well for *her*.

"I tell you that I love you," Noah said, "but you hardly ever say the same to me."

"Look, I'll admit that I'm not as expressive as you are," Devon answered. "But I'm starting to think that maybe the way we've always explained things isn't exactly fair to me. Since we started talking I've realized that I *do* want something from you. I still don't know exactly what that is, but I know I'm not getting it from all your 'I love yous.' When you tell me how beautiful I am it just doesn't mean that much to me."

"How can 'I love you' not mean anything?" a frustrated Noah asked.

"Maybe because I don't feel you're really talking about *me*," Devon answered.

"How could 'I love you' not be about you?"

"Because you never ask me really basic questions, like 'How are you?' Because it's easier for you to give me diamond earrings than it is to clear your dishes off the table, even though I've asked you a million times. You know what's a big thing? You never use my name. You call me 'sweetie' and 'honey,' but you never call me 'Devon.'" Devon paused for a moment, and then, her voice softening, added: "I do believe that you love me, but sometimes I don't feel like you really know me. And when it comes right down to it, I think I'd rather have you know me than love me."

This book argues that we have deep and inbred capacities to change and grow, and that taking shared, creative risks with someone loved and trusted enhances these capacities. But let's not fool ourselves—marriage is hard. And if there is one single factor that makes our marriages hard, it is that they become crucibles for our own individual pain. All of us come from places of hurt and injury, and all of us, in one way or another, conscript our intimate partners into shouldering the burden of our own wounds.

Noah and Devon were no exception.

Noah's mother died suddenly and unexpectedly from an aortic aneurysm when he was thirteen. "It was the August before I started high school," he told us. "I remember it was a really hot day, and I had been playing baseball down the street with some friends. An ambulance drove by, sirens blaring, lights flashing, and everything. We all got on our bikes and chased it. It stopped in front of my house. There was a policeman at my door, and he wouldn't let me in. From there things get kind of hazy. I remember them taking my mother out on a stretcher, I think I remember her face was gray, and I vaguely remember going in the police car to the hospital. I definitely remember the doctor telling us she was dead.

"For the next ten years I felt like a zombie," Noah continued, the monotone of his voice an eerie counterpoint to the gravity of what he was saying. "My father was a nice guy, a doctor, great at his work, but he never really knew what to do with us kids. It was my mother who held everything together. She worked too, but she was the one who made meals, did the laundry, tucked us in, knew who our friends were—all that stuff. I don't think we ever got over her death. After she was gone my sister, my brother, my father, and I were like roommates. We'd get up in the morning, have a bowl of cereal, make a peanut butter sandwich, my dad would go off to the hospital, us kids would head off to school. At night someone would order take-out. We just stopped being a family."

The "zombie-like" feeling, as Noah called it, continued when he went off to college, and then through medical school. "I probably became a doctor because my father was a doctor, not because medicine was my great passion. On looking back I was pretty much just putting one foot in front of the other."

Then, during his residency, Noah and Devon were introduced by mutual friends. Never serious about relationships, never having thought about having a family, Noah wanted to marry Devon within a few months of meeting her. "I felt alive for the first time since my mother died. I loved Devon as much as I ever loved anybody, as much as I loved my mother, I guess. But as the years went by I realized that Devon didn't love me back the way my mother did."

And Devon, it was clear, was paying a high price for not loving Noah in the way that he imagined his mother had loved him.

KEEPING OURSELVES SAFE BY TAKING EACH OTHER FOR GRANTED

It is an uncanny aspect of romantic attraction that we fall in love with others who are, both for better and for worse, seamless fits with our deepest and most hidden fault lines and vulnerabilities. In the beginning the match seems to be for the better. If we haven't had solid and trustworthy parents we believe we have finally found a partner on whom we can rely. If we are missing a certain sense of liveliness in our own selves, we find it through our new love. If we are disorganized, we find a lover who organizes us. And so it goes; these seemingly serendipitous counterpoints are all in the nature of what we call "chemistry." Then, as romance fades and as we see our partners in an increasingly human, and, it often follows, disappointing light, the "for worse" sets in. We find the flakiness beneath our lovers' stability. We learn about the anxiety that fuels their liveliness. We find their orderliness to be stodgy and controlling. In these ways, and many more, we learn that our lovers' leading, positive edges are often compensations for their shortcomings, and with this our once-healing soul mates seem to become the sources of, rather than the antidotes to, our pain.

And so love presents us with a relentless paradox: on the one hand, intimacy allows us to touch each other in those parts of ourselves that are most in need of healing. On the other hand, love causes us to wound each other in those places that we can least afford to be wounded.

Consider what happened when Noah met Devon. He found her physically beautiful, to be sure, and also warm, funny, and reliable. Here, he imagined, was a woman whom he could love, who could love him, and whom he could trust not to leave him. He emerged from the numbness in which he had wrapped himself since his mother's death, and he took the monumental risk of allowing himself to want and need in places he had long ago locked away.

But then reality, alas, intervened. What Noah had felt to be Devon's strength he came to see as her distance, and where he had seen her to be solid he began to find her impassive. Noah had taken a risk by loving Devon and had gotten hurt, and as time went by he had, largely without admitting it to himself, grown increasingly angry and disappointed.

So how did a now-injured Noah deal with his pain? By doing something that we all do, to greater or lesser degrees, when the spell of romantic idealization begins to wear thin, and when we wake up to the fact that we now love and depend on a real-life person who has the power to truly hurt us. He made her, in the words of American psychoanalyst Stephen Mitchell, into a "habit."[1] He took her for granted, thus subtly but effectively neutralizing her separate, unpredictable (and therefore dangerous to him) self.

And he did so in the everyday ways that undermine so many of our intimate relationships.

For all of his apparent openness, for all of his protestations of love, Noah was in fact as reserved and withholding as his wife, the self-proclaimed "cold WASP bitch." He claimed that he understood her, but the truth was that he wasn't very good at simply listening to what *she* said about herself. He considered himself to be open and sensitive, but he was in fact quite stubborn when it came to doing the simple things that made her feel cared about: coordinating better about the children, cleaning up after himself, and keeping track of what she had done during the course of her day. And while he frequently sang her praises, an undercurrent of criticism ran beneath his flowery compliments; when one read between the lines one could hear Noah calling his wife a cold, uptight, and unloving woman.

Noah had come to view his wife almost exclusively through the lens of his own wishes and fears. His preemptive assumption that she was unable to love him excused him from the risk of knowing her as a real and separate—in other words different—person. No wonder Devon often felt that her husband didn't really know her.

Understanding Devon's Reserve

For the first several months of our work together I tried to show Noah that he had his own form of "reserve," one that was as hurtful to Devon as was hers to him. I noted that his relationship with his mother had never been reconfigured by the realism that comes from seeing one's parents through adult eyes; how, I asked, could Devon possibly compete with a memory, particularly one that lived enshrined in a state of cryogenic perfection?

I showed him the ways in which Devon was right in her assertion that, for all of his proclamations of love, he didn't seem to know her very well. We all see our partners through the prisms of our own histories, I noted, but Noah needed to struggle more actively to understand that the real-life Devon differed from the one he had constructed from his wishes, fears, and expectations.

And finally, I urged Noah to better tolerate his deep-seated fear of loss. "You're scared that if you let her be real with you, and if you're in turn real with her, then she'll be able to hurt you," I said. "If you want her to feel closer to you you'll have to deal with that fear."

Noah found my one-sided persistence irritating, but he did genuinely love his wife, and he cared about making their relationship better. He pushed himself to let go of his assumptions about Devon and to be more open to his own vulnerabilities and insecurities. Devon, in turn, rewarded Noah's willingness to be honest with himself by putting the subject of her "reserve" squarely on the table.

Devon, we learned, had as much reason to fear being hurt as did Noah. One of three children, she had been the only daughter, and she had been her father's favorite. "He'd bring me presents when he came home from work, tell me how wonderful I was, tuck me in every night," she said. "My brothers joked about how he loved me more than them, and my mother would get mad at him for spoiling me, but the world really felt pretty cozy when I was little."

Then, dramatically and unexpectedly, things changed; when Devon was thirteen her father had left her mother for another woman. "After my father left I visited him every other weekend for a while, but then even that stopped. The last straw came when I was nineteen, and I was home from college. I was walking through town and I saw him hand in hand with this little girl. I swear to God for a moment I felt like I was out of my own body watching the way he and I used to be. It turned out it was his new five-year-old daughter. I wanted to cry, but all I could do was feel totally humiliated and go eat the biggest bowl of ice cream I could find."

"My father's love turned out to be a bunch of bullshit," Devon concluded. "He just traded us in like a used car. That's why I react the way I do to Noah's 'I love yous.' We've been together for fifteen years now, and I still don't know if I can trust that he really cares about me."

Devon, like Noah, had entered the marriage wounded by a childhood loss. And like her husband, she lessened her fear of being hurt again by hiding behind strategically inaccurate assumptions about her spouse. Sure, Noah kept his distance in complicated and hurtful ways, but he was also basically trustworthy, he loved his wife, and he wanted to be loved in return. By focusing on Noah's sometimes flowery and superficial proclamations of love while overlooking the decency and vulnerability that lay beneath, Devon justified her reserve. After all, how foolish would it be to once again trust a man who claimed that he loved her, but who could just as easily "trade her in like a used car"?

Noah and Devon's relationship had become organized around the principle of "Who you don't know can't hurt you," with each member of the couple embracing a partial and inaccurate understanding of the other in order to justify his or her distance. If things were going to get better they would have to risk encountering each other as real and separate people. They would have to replace the safe but closed system that they had created with the creative friction that comes from risking being open, vulnerable, and honest with each other.

MARRIED MINDS AND CHANGING BRAINS: "LIFE TEACHES US WHO WE ARE."

Recognize, and then celebrate, your differences; in many ways the entire enterprise of growing through long-lasting intimacy revolves around this principle. By appreciating the ways that our lovers differ from ourselves (and, importantly, from our self-protective assumptions and expectations), we are able to heal old wounds, to improve our relationships, and to change and enliven our selves.

There is a growing body of contemporary research that supports the argument that we grow through being open to each other's differences. At the core of this research lie some fascinating findings about the physiological changes that take place in our brains as we learn.

In 2000, Columbia University neuroscientist Eric Kandel won the Nobel Prize in medicine for his work on how sea slugs learn.[2] Among other breakthroughs, Kandel's work demonstrated that new experience (in the case of Kandel's sea slugs, a small electric jolt) leads to observable, permanent changes in the biological systems that govern learning. And while we should of course be cautious in generalizing from sea slugs to human beings, Kandel's work has become a focal point for a growing body of knowledge regarding how we learn and remember. Not merely how we learn and remember new skills and new facts, but how we change and grow at the deepest levels of our essential selves.[3]

Here's how.

Every experience that befalls a person makes its mark on the mind's circuitry, the ten billion or so neural cells with which we are born.[4] Metaphorically speaking, our brains undergo a process that is similar to the way water carves grooves in the sand, grooves that in turn cause subsequent rivulets of water to flow in the same pattern.[5] As the mind collects a library of experience, certain of our neurons, and then certain groups of our neurons, become programmed to fire in predictable patterns in response to similar and familiar experiences. These groupings, which are called "neural networks," organize and express our mental histories, and therefore our selves.

This kind of programmed learning can be seen in the scripts and expectations that Noah and Devon brought into their marriage. For both Noah and Devon, love had led to loss, and once the buffering magic of early romance wore off, the couple experienced each other through this time-worn mental groove. Just as Kandel literally changed the neurology of his sea slugs when he taught them that a gentle nudge would be followed by an electric shock (they learned to recoil from the anticipated shock even when given only the nudge), the wiring of Noah and Devon's neurologies led both to assume that loving would bring them to pain. This assumption caused both to recoil into self-protective shells, and then caused each to interpret the other's withdrawal as further evidence that love invariably leads to heartache.

All of this could sound pretty discouraging. If we enter our relationships programmed to see our partners through the distorting prisms of our pasts, how do we ever get to know each other? How do we ever change? Fortunately, relationship fault lines can be transformed into relationship opportunities. Just as our painful histories are a prime culprit in making long-term intimacy a challenge, long-term intimacy, in turn, has the power to free us from the grip of those painful histories.

The physiology of new learning gives us a window into how this can happen.

While every experience makes some mark on the mind simply because every experience, indeed every perception, every action, and every thought, causes a neuron or pattern of neurons to fire, when it comes to learning, some experiences are "more equal" than others. Repeated experiences, experiences with important and loved people, and experiences that occur in an atmosphere of highly charged emotion make more indelible marks on the brain.[6]

Sound familiar? Long-term intimate relationships are filled with interactions of heightened emotional intensity. These interactions occur repeatedly in relationships as the same elemental scripts play again and again. And intimate relationships occur, obviously, between important and loved people. Add it all up and it becomes clear that the experiences that occur in our intimate relationships are precisely the kinds that lead to the creation of the most enduring and influential neural pathways.

The downside of all this is that when we repeat old scripts in our relationships we powerfully reinforce old pathways and patterns. But there is also a significant upside. What happens when we open ourselves to the ways in which our partners *diverge* from those old patterns? When we experience the ways that they *differ* from our ingrained assumptions and expectations? Simply put, we rewire our brains, we rewrite old scripts, and so we change and grow on the deepest, most personal level of our selves.

Salman Rushdie writes: "Our lives teach us who we are."[7] His words are the literary counterpart to those of neuroscientist Thomas Lewis, who writes: "Experience rewires the microscopic structures of the brain—transforming us from who we were to who we are."[8] Noah and Devon were hurting, to be sure, but in their pain they also possessed the opportunity to learn and grow in precisely the ways referred to by Rushdie and Lewis; by changing their relationship they could change each other's brains,[9] and so also change each other's selves.[10]

Noah and Devon: An Exercise in Real Intimacy

Noah and Devon made these changes by trading in the safety of their long-held arrangements for the risk of being real with each other. They learned to see each other more accurately, and then they used their newfound acuity to replace old scripts related to loss and betrayal with new scripts associated with hope and trust. And they did all of this by playing together in their most core and most vulnerable places.

As was the case with Michael and Susan, much of this play took place in bed.

When it came to sex Noah was, as he was elsewhere, a complex mixture of idealization and criticism. On the one hand he spoke in rapturous terms about how beautiful and exciting he found Devon, but at the same time he subtly criticized his wife by implying that she was sexually unresponsive. He typically couched his complaints in sympathy and concern ("It must be hard for her to be so cut off from herself sexually"), but by now Devon had left behind the idea that she was a "cold WASP bitch" and she wasn't buying.

"It always looks like he does everything right," she objected, her voice rising in irritation. "When it comes to sex it's always about what I want, about what feels good to me, like he's this selfless lover. I'll admit, he *does* care about what feels good to me sexually. But sex seems antiseptic—sometimes I feel like he might just as well be doing a really good job of brushing my teeth. And this stuff about my supposedly great body, well, I'm a forty-five-year-old woman with two kids, and those perfect breasts he's talking about are a thing of the past."

"Sometimes I have no clue what you want," Noah shot back.

"How can you turn my caring about what feels good to you into a bad thing?"

"Because I don't feel like you're there emotionally," Devon answered, keeping her cool. "When it comes to sex I think your mind follows your body. For me it's the other way—my body follows my mind. I need to trust you for sex to feel good, and I need to feel like we know each other if I'm going to trust you."

Once again the matter of knowing each other as real and separate people came to the forefront. When it came to sex, Noah treated Devon as Galatea to his Pygmalion; as largely a construction of his own mind. And once Devon sensed Noah's retreat, she withdrew. I suggested an exercise.

"How about the next time you make love you pay as much attention to what's going on in Devon's mind as you do to what's going on in her body?" I said, speaking directly to Noah. "This may sound a bit corny, but what if you try to remember that when she was a little girl her father left her? What if you make a point of reminding yourself that she's less cold than she is scared?"

"It's corny, but it sounds okay," Noah answered. Then, after a moment's pause he added: "But can I interrupt this one-sided therapy of yours with a request?"

"Fair enough," I laughed, appreciating Noah's lightly bantering tone.

"How about if this goes both ways? How about if she remembers that *my* life wasn't so easy when I was a kid, and that *I* need a little love and understanding too?"

We had a deal, and over the next several months Noah and Devon used the occasion of going to bed to continue the conversations that they had begun in my office. They talked about their childhoods, about what they really wanted from each other, and about what it felt like to let down their guard. They talked about misunderstandings they had had during the week.

They talked about the mundane as well—what they had done during the day, and what the kids were up to. And in an important departure from what took place in my office, they talked while lying in each other's arms. They found these conversations exciting, but also a little dangerous.

"Want to know what the strangest part of all this is for me?" Noah asked, several weeks after beginning this playful ritual. "How different sex feels. I've always liked sex, but in some way, like everything else in my life, I've always been half outside myself watching. Now when we make love I feel her skin, the way she moves, her breath; sometimes it almost feels like she's too real."

"Too real?" I asked.

"Yeah. So what do I mean by that? I guess I realize that I could lose her. That she'll die someday. God, is that morbid."

"Not really. More like what you first said—'real,'" I answered.

"I feel like we've gone from Pygmalion to *The Velveteen Rabbit*," Devon laughed, referencing the children's story about a stuffed rabbit that becomes frayed but "real" by virtue of its child-owner's consistent love. Then she continued, her tone becoming more pensive: "I like being real in his mind, I've been asking for that. But I'm scared too. I have this repeating worry that Noah will trade me in just like my father did."

I asked Devon what she meant.

"Part of me is beginning to trust him, but another part of me says: 'Here he is, this good-looking nice-guy pediatrician who talks a really good game. What will keep him from just getting someone new and improved?'" Turning to her husband, Devon continued: "Why wouldn't you choose someone new and easy over someone who has all this baggage attached?"

"Because I love you," Noah answered.

Devon shifted uncomfortably. Noah's "I love you" hadn't hit the mark.

"That's where you lose her," I broke in. "You mean what you say, but she doesn't quite trust it. Remember, she's looking for something different from those 'I love yous.'"

"I'm working on it," Noah answered. "But I do have one complaint in all this. I *like* telling her I love her. I *like* finding her beautiful. I don't just do it for her, I do it for me. Can't I say those things anymore?"

"Maybe I have to work on letting you feel that way," Devon answered, after a moment's pause. Then she added ironically: "Boy that's really big of me, working on letting my husband tell me he loves me. Every woman should have problems like mine, right?"

With this Devon's voice turned serious. "It sounds stupid, but it does still scare me when you say you love me. It scares me less than it used to, but it still scares me. Maybe that will keep changing, though. Maybe the more I trust that you know me the more I'll trust that I won't come crashing down when you put me on that pedestal of yours."

Following this exchange Noah, Devon, and I met for a few more months. Our talks focused on how their shared fear of loss had shaped their minds and their relationship. And in talking about this fear we thought together about what may well be the core challenge of creative aging: how to find meaning not despite the constraints and limitations that govern our lives, but *through* them. Noah and Devon's worst fear *would* eventually be realized: when it comes to love and relationships permanence is an illusion; all love ends in loss. The solution, therefore, does not lie in trying to avoid loss, but in accepting its eventuality in order to better appreciate the moments that we have.

Here is what Devon had to say in our final session: "The other day we went out for ice cream, just the two of us for a change. We were walking down the street, Noah took my hand, and all of a sudden I flashed back to that time I saw my father with his new daughter. I thought about how everything can be taken away from you without any warning. But then I thought about Noah, and I realized that I trust him."

"I've probably cried more in the past two years than I did the whole time since I was twenty," Devon continued, "but I also think I'm learning how to be less scared."

SOME PRACTICAL STEPS TO A STRONGER (AND LESS SELF-CENTERED) SELF

We grow through our willingness to touch, even at times to collide with, our partners' real-life selves. By recognizing and then appreciating the ways in which our lovers differ from our assumptions and expectations, we learn to rewrite old, self-protective scripts, thus changing ourselves in those places that are most injured, most cloistered, and most in need of change. Our spouses, if we are open to them, teach us who we are, and our increased self-knowledge, in turn, helps us to become our best selves.

Noah and Devon, like most of the couples described in this book, got better with the help of therapy. To repeat an earlier point, however, I mean for therapy to be a lens, not a central character. You don't necessarily need to be in therapy to make your life better. But whether or not you are in therapy you do need to pursue, persistently and proactively, the same basic principles of change.

Here are some guidelines that can help us to recognize, and then celebrate, our differences.

- **Talk to each other.** *Really talk* to each other. Sometimes we learn more from talking with someone for three hours on an airplane than when we talk with our spouses, simply because we take the time to really talk and really listen. So talk to each other as if you don't know each other (which ultimately you don't) and keep doing that over the course of your relationship.

- **When it comes to talking, make a point of bringing things up when things are *good*.** Talking only when things are hard is one of the most common errors we make in our relationships. When things are good we often don't bring up hard subjects because we don't want to rock the boat. But good times are in fact the *best* time to talk. When we feel good with each other we say what we have to say thoughtfully, and we are also able to hear each other better.

- **Be aware of those places in which you are brittle and vulnerable, and know that when you are speaking from those places you are unlikely to be your best self.** And when you stumble into those more brittle and vulnerable places in your partner, extend to them the same tenderness that you would wish to have extended to you.

- **Learn to recognize your own familiar scripts.** Be clear about the ways that you assume your partner fits into these scripts, and then get to know the ways that he or she actually diverges from your expectations and assumptions.

- **Know the familiar relationship "don'ts":** externalization, blame, denigration, rationalization, and even idealization. Understand that each of these undermines our relationships by allowing us to make our partners into safe but familiar "habits."

- **Revel in your partner's unknowability.** If you appreciate how much there is that you don't know about each other, your relationship will never get stale.

And if you need to take the lead in the hope that your partner will follow suit:

- **Don't analyze your partner;** instead focus on how much you don't know about yourself.
- **Substitute kindness for judgment.** Don't judge, period.
- Once again, **set an example.** Model, and wait for your partner to follow.
- Finally and above all, **don't try to change your partner.** Instead take love's ultimate risk: let yourself be changed.

Celebrate your differences. If you do this you may find, to your great surprise, that two of the most interesting people you'll meet in your advancing years are persons you thought you already knew: your spouse—and yourself.

One final note.

As is the case with each of the eight resolutions outlined in these pages, these guidelines are meant to help us build a shared and private space in which we can grow and change through intimacy's creative friction. They are meant to help us become our best selves.

"To help us become our best selves." Now seems a good time to revisit the premise that "making our relationships work for us" is *not* a self-centered ambition. Indeed, our long-term, intimate relationships are, at their best, powerful *antidotes* to narcissism.

Here's how.

Narcissism involves covering up feelings of helplessness, inadequacy, and shame with the irritating (to others) symptoms of omnipotence, entitlement, arrogance, control, blame, grievance, and denigration. These symptoms allow us to deflect responsibility for our troubles and disappointments ("It's not my fault that our relationship stinks, it's yours"), to construct a false but reassuring sense of self-esteem ("I'm special, even if nobody seems to recognize it"), and to wrap ourselves in a reassuring but illusory sense of omnipotence and control ("Of course I'm right about what's happening between us; after all, I'm a psychologist").

Narcissism, when all is said and done, leaves us standing on a three-legged throne of grandiosity and self-centeredness in an effort to mask deep-seated feelings of being worthless and unlovable.

More than any other means available to us, our long-term relationships can counter narcissism's self-defeating self-centeredness.

When we tie ourselves in, lean back, and let go, when we are willing to reveal to each other the most vulnerable layers of ourselves, we encounter, through the separate and nonnegotiable realities of each other, truths that lie outside of our control. When we are exposed to these truths in an environment of kindness and compassion (as occurs in a trusting and loving relationship), we learn to appreciate the fact that the world is not merely our own personal oyster. A good relationship, therefore, can serve as a kind of "reality with training wheels"; when we relentlessly discipline ourselves to recognize each other's differences, and when we then challenge ourselves to celebrate those same differences, we can disabuse ourselves of the notion that the subjective—how we wish things to be—should trump the objective—how things really are.

"Making our relationships work for us," it follows, is not an exercise in narcissism. It is a high-risk and high-reward exercise in building a more centered, and less *self*-centered, self.

TWO KIDS AND TEN POUNDS

"Are you sure you want that?" As soon as the words were out, Kurt had wanted to stuff them back. But there was no going back on either the words or the tone; the reddening in Megan's face made it clear that she had heard his reaction to the ice-cream sundae she had just ordered.

The kid behind the counter finished up their children's order, then asked if she wanted whipped cream with the sundae. "You know, I don't think I want anything after all," Megan had answered. Her tone was stiffly formal, the way it always was when she was trying not to show that she was hurt. "I'll just have a cup of water, please."

"Have the sundae," Kurt had urged. "You can handle it. Besides, it's none of my business."

"You're right, I don't need it," she'd answered, but he knew that the only part that she really felt he was right about was the "none of my business" part.

"I'm really sorry," Kurt said later that night, as they lay across from each other on the bed. "I shouldn't have said that stuff about the ice cream. But maybe we could both stand to watch what we eat."

"Don't start giving me that 'I'm just trying to be helpful' crap, Kurt," Megan shot back. "You know how much more I weigh than the day we met? Ten pounds. That's five pounds for each kid. For each of your kids, by the way."

Ten pounds? Was that all? It sure felt like more than ten pounds. He missed the way her body felt before the kids were born, the way her shoulders once felt small and slight in his hands. Now they were strong, mostly from the yoga, he supposed, but even though she was in good shape there was something different about her body that "ten pounds" just didn't capture.

Kurt looked back at his wife, and she caught his glance. "Ten pounds," she said. "Two kids and ten pounds. I wonder what you'd look like if you'd had two kids?"

Kurt was silent. He knew that his wife was right; that she took care of her body, and that what she chose to eat was really none of his business anyway. But while one part of his mind told him to let it all go, another told him to hold on as tight as he could, that something really big was at stake, even if he couldn't quite see what that was.

"Don't you think it's fair to help each other with stuff like this?" he asked tentatively. "I wouldn't mind if you wanted me to stay in shape."

Megan was having none of it. "No, Kurt, I don't think it's fair. First of all, the idea that I can talk to you about stuff that is supposedly good for you is bullshit. What happens when I tell you I think you drive too fast? You basically act like I'm castrating you. And don't tell me this is about helping *me*. This is about you confusing me with your mother for the ten thousandth time."

The mention of Kurt's mother jarred him. He realized that she had been strangely absent from his mind throughout the conversation; "strangely" because it seemed obvious that talking with his wife about her eating and her weight would take him back to the woman who had probably been a pretty good mother until he was about five, but who then had seemed to give up on her life. "With her it was more like four kids and a hundred pounds," he thought wryly to himself. "Twenty-five pounds a kid." And it wasn't just the weight. He could still picture her sitting on the couch, watching television in that ratty nightgown until noon, the diabetes-induced sores blossoming on her legs.

Kurt looked at his wife and smiled. It occurred to him that he probably knew her too well to ever see her with real clarity, but there was something about picturing her next to his mother that brought her more into focus. Indeed, he had learned that he had to keep an eye on where his mother was in his head: when he lost track of her she seemed to come to life through his wife, and then he became that controlling, micromanaging pain in the ass that she complained about.

Megan knew from Kurt's smile that she had gained a foothold, and she dug in further: "I remember the first time I met her. I remember thinking about that old saying that guys look to marry their mothers. I wondered what it was you could possibly see in me that reminded you of her."

"I know you're nothing like her," Kurt said. "Thank God. Look, I'm sorry about that stuff earlier."

"Don't worry about it. Sometimes I confuse *you* with my *father*."

"You mean the slick used-car salesman who tried to sleaze out of paying for your wedding?"

"Exactly," Megan answered, rolling over and turning out the light.

CHAPTER III

HAVE REAL SEX

Jeremy and Margaret, married for nineteen years, came to talk with me because they wanted to learn to "communicate better." Mostly the work we did was pretty basic. Listen more carefully. Speak more directly. Talk about your own feelings. Don't criticize. Don't interpret. Don't judge. The couple had a solid relationship, they were committed to making things better, they worked at talking to each other, and after about six months they felt that they had gotten the help that they wanted.

"But maybe before we stop we could run one last thing by you," Margaret asked, speaking with uncharacteristic shyness.

"Sure," I answered, eager to hear.

"Can we talk about sex?"

"Absolutely."

Jeremy and Margaret shared a nervous glance, and then Margaret began: "I feel like we have a pretty good sex life; I think Jeremy does too. But the other day we were talking, and, well—it seems like these days everyone is doing everything and anything with everybody. We both were teenagers in the seventies, but this is different. Even kids—our oldest is in eighth grade now, and apparently they have classmates who are already having intercourse. Is that really true?"

I told Jeremy and Margaret that the sexual landscape for

young kids had indeed undergone a seismic shift—that even kids who weren't having sex were far more immersed in a culture of explicit sexuality than was the case fifteen, even ten, years previously. I wondered what this meant to them.

"Our sex life *is* pretty good," Jeremy joined in. "But I hear about what everyone else seems to be doing, and sometimes—I dunno—it seems like there's a big party going on out there and we're the only ones who didn't get invited. Are we missing something?"

Jeremy is hardly alone in feeling left out of the party. These days it can seem as if everyone is having wild and fantastic sex, and lots of it. A deeper look, however, tells us that the party, if there even is one, is a lot less fun than it appears.

Let's start with the somewhat jarring example that Jeremy mentioned: our kids. Oral sex and even intercourse are indeed common practices among fourteen-year-olds, twelve-year-olds, and even younger children. That these children are so young is disturbing,[1] but while these precocious sexual practices are admittedly headline-grabbers, they aren't the only, or even the biggest, problem. What's more troubling is what kids are feeling about the sex that they're having: "It's just a thing to do," they say, particularly when referring to oral sex. "It doesn't mean anything."

As the terms "friends with benefits" and "hooking up" suggest, sex for many youngsters has become a disengaged and impersonal act.

Adults, meanwhile, are similarly beset with feelings of sexual disconnection. Husbands and wives are often disappointed in their partners; cosmetic surgery and devotion to physical fitness don't give us bodies that are attractive enough; we depend on Viagra, male-enhancement surgery, and other forms of sexual technology to insure our potency and performance, and "sex addicts" (to use the now-common parlance) are driven from sexual experience to sexual experience without ever being sated.

When one really talks to people about their sexual lives it becomes clear that many of us are not particularly happy or satisfied.

Is it really possible to be sexually alienated and unhappy when living in a society in which advertisements, television, magazines, billboards, movies, the Internet, and the increasingly mainstream multibillion-dollar pornography industry tell us that we can and should have our sex whenever and however we want—a society that suggests that great sex all the time is an entitlement, and if we're missing out, well, there are lots of enviable others who aren't?

It's not only possible, it's inevitable. Here's why.

For starters, there is the matter of *how much* sex we are surrounded by. We may think we've grown accustomed to our hypersexual environment, but what we believe to be acclimation can more accurately be understood as the result of our minds becoming numb in order to protect us from an overstimulating barrage. This numbing is lightly reminiscent of the sexual experience of victims of sexual abuse: sex for them is often frightening and invasive, but it is also, quite frequently, disengaged and without pleasure. As one woman said to me: "The worst thing my father did when he abused me was he stole my sexuality. When I make love with my husband I feel like a zombie."

To say that we have become a nation of sexual zombies probably goes too far, but to say that we are being numbed by sexual overstimulation does not.

Then there is the matter of *what kind* of sex surrounds us. There is an enormous gap between the "great" sex that we are all supposed to be having and the real sex that we are actually capable of having. Just as the unattainable images of attractiveness that surround us often leave us unhappy with our bodies and with the bodies of our partners, our culture's message of unlimited sexual possibility can alienate us from those same partners, and, on a deeper level, from our own sexual selves.

The sexual freedom and permissiveness in which we baby boomers once reveled has evolved into a sexual culture that now, ironically, shackles and oppresses us.[2]

Is there any way out of this mess?

Once again, our long-term intimate relationships can provide us with a solution; in this case the opportunity to find and sustain our sexualities in the face of what is fast becoming an epidemic of sexual meaninglessness and disconnection.

Have real sex. This is the third resolution. Sex with someone whom we know and who in turn knows us; sex with someone whose separateness and difference we recognize and appreciate; sex in a long-term, intimate relationship—sex such as this can help us to find and sustain healthy sexual selves. And, even more impressively, such sex can do so in a society that alienates us from all that is good and meaningful about sex.

DAN AND MELISSA JACOBSON

"We don't want this to take forever," Dan Jacobson said. "There isn't a whole lot we need to understand, mostly we just need to decide whether or not to get a divorce." Dan appeared to be in his mid-fifties. His suit was impeccably tailored, accentuating his still well-muscled build. His receding hair was carefully combed, though the telltale plugs of a hair transplant were easily noticeable. He didn't look young, but he was obviously quite fit.

Dan's wife, Melissa, nodded, less in agreement than in tired acknowledgment. This appeared to be Dan's agenda, not hers.

I turned to Melissa. "Do you have the same question?"

Melissa shifted her glance from her husband, at whom she had been staring intently, to me. She, too, wore expensive clothes, though she seemed at odds with her outward appearance, as if she were wearing a familiar but somewhat uncomfortable uniform.

"For me it's always been about whether or not I'd be able to make Dan happy," she answered, after a moment's pause. Then, grimacing at her words, she added: "God, that makes me sound pathetic. It's more that I do what I can, I know it won't be good enough, and I try not to worry too much about it."

"You know before you even start that what you do won't be good enough?" I asked.

"Yes. At least when it comes to the reason that we're here." Melissa glanced warily at her husband. "Most of this—no, all of this— is about sex. He's very dissatisfied with our sex life. He's felt that way for the whole twenty-five years that we've been married."

"That's a long time," I noted.

"She's right," Dan added, his tone resigned.

"So if it's been twenty-five years, what's the rush to make a decision?" I asked.

"Well," he answered, "I'm not exactly getting any younger. But I guess we're here because we owe it to each other to talk things over with someone for a bit."

Dan and Melissa did owe each other some thoughtful talk. Dan's intimation of divorce notwithstanding, their twenty-five years of marriage had been twenty-five pretty good years. The couple had one child, a daughter who had recently graduated from college. They had supported each other in building successful careers; Dan had been in on the ground floor of a couple of high-tech start-ups, and Melissa ran her own head-hunting firm. Dan, for all his complaints about sex, had been faithful to Melissa over the years, and he appreciated her mind ("I think she's a lot smarter than I am"), her mothering ("a heck of a lot more nurturing than me"), and her wit ("sometimes we just can't stop laughing").

Melissa, in turn, felt that Dan was her best friend. "I'm shy," she said, "and he's really the person closest to me."

"Most of the time we put the stuff about sex aside, and we

get along well," Melissa explained. "But then every couple of months he tells me he can't go on like this. He's like Halley's Comet, only more frequent. It used to be that when he started to talk about divorce I would cry for days, but now I've almost gotten used to it."

Dan, Melissa, and I began to meet weekly. For the most part Dan *was* a reasonable man, but when the subject turned to sex he battered Melissa with his endless complaints. First there was the matter of Melissa's body; she didn't work hard enough to keep herself in shape. Then there was the quality of their orgasms; making love should always be a "peak" experience, as Dan called it. There was the matter of variety; Melissa wasn't adventurous enough, they should watch pornography together and try out the positions the pros used. And of course then there was the problem of frequency; four or five times a week, in Dan's estimation, was nowhere near enough, even for a couple of fifty-five-year-olds.

At first I listened patiently to Dan's litany of demands. I watched him grow increasingly upset as he listed his grievances, and I watched Melissa's eyes glaze over for what I imagined to be the umpteenth time in their relationship. I wondered silently about the content of Dan's seemingly nonnegotiable needs, imagining that they might reflect struggles with his masculinity, with his feelings about growing older, with his fear of being vulnerable, but I set these thoughts aside; I imagined that sharing them would only make Dan feel defensive. Instead I asked Dan about a less obvious element of his frustration:

"Dan," I said, hoping that my voice was firm enough to interrupt the disembodied, ritualized flow of his complaints. "I understand that these are things you feel you really need. But you're talking about sex with another person. Melissa. Where does how she feels and what she wants fit into all this?"

"I pay a lot of attention to what makes her feel good," Dan answered defensively.

"I'm not talking about what feels good to her body. I'm talking about her as a person."

To my surprise, Dan became quite thoughtful, and when he answered, his tone seemed more engaged: "I'm not so aware of her as a person when we have sex. It's like I'm in a different state of mind than at other times in our relationship."

Often during the first few months of what would become a two-year therapy, our sessions followed this same pattern. Dan would complain about sex while Melissa sat silently; a man reciting a gospel so familiar that its meaning was all but lost. After a few minutes I would interrupt Dan's sermonizing: "We know all this," I'd say, firm but a bit impatient. "But look—sex is *always* an intimate reflection of who a person is, his struggles and his solutions. I wonder what all this means about *you?*"

With my interruption Dan's tone and demeanor would shift, and he would talk with surprising openness about his obsession with sex and with his body. He talked about how he ran, dieted, and lifted weights. About how he took supplements to increase his muscle mass. About how he masturbated daily, always looking at himself in the mirror as he did, searching for imperfections. And he spoke about how he took Viagra in order to heighten his sexual responsiveness, even though he had never had any erectile dysfunction.

Increasingly, however, Dan's obsessions were failing to bring him satisfaction, so much so that even *he* began to tire of his complaints. By the third month of our sessions he said: "Sometimes I wish Melissa would just stop me. When I get on one of my rolls I don't even think about what I'm saying. It's like I feel I need all this stuff I'm asking for just to be OK."

"To be OK?"

"Yeah. I don't know exactly what I mean by that, but that's what it feels like."

Dan's openness allowed Melissa to enter the conversation more fully. "I know this is going to upset Dan," she said, "but sex doesn't really matter to me anymore. He works hard at making it good for me, I have orgasms most of the time, but for me sex is probably the least important part of our relationship. It's like it's something that I give him, while I live my real life somewhere else."

Melissa was by no means "pathetic," as she feared she appeared. She was an intelligent and strong woman, and, in contrast to her husband, she understood what lay behind her long-standing arrangements. Her parents had been critical of every blemish, every extra pound, every grade less than a straight A. Over time she had learned to hide from her parents' criticism in much the same way she now hid from Dan's; she gave her parents what they wanted while keeping her more personal thoughts and feelings private. And now, in her relationship with Dan, she had constructed a similarly intricate system of barter. She tried to give her husband what *he* wanted, all the while knowing that what she was offering wasn't really her.

"Finally when I reached fifty I decided that I was fine," Melissa said. "Not perfect, but good enough. That was a big deal. It would be wonderful to feel that I'm good enough for Dan too, but I've resigned myself to not having that. Dan doesn't really know who I am sexually, so his criticisms don't really get to me."

Melissa's words got through to Dan. He could hear that he was losing her, and on top of that he was becoming increasingly unhappy with himself. "I guess I have to go about things differently," he told us. "But to be honest, I've been this way for a long time, and I don't really know how to change."

WHAT IS HEALTHY SEXUALITY?
(SOLVING POTTER STEWART'S DILEMMA)

In order for Dan and Melissa's sexual relationship to improve, Melissa needed to risk becoming more sexually open with her husband. In order for Melissa to take that risk Dan needed to become less controlling and obsessive. And in order for Dan to make this change he needed to develop a healthier relationship with sex.

Sounds good, but what do we mean by "a healthier relationship with sex"? Let's approach this question by way of an old debate; that regarding the difference between erotic art and pornography.

A number of years ago Supreme Court Justice Potter Stewart faced the daunting proposition of articulating a legal definition of "pornography." His now-famous answer—"I know it when I see it"—is an evocative one, but Justice Stewart could have been more precise had he referenced the French psychoanalyst Joyce McDougall's discussion of erotica and pornography. "Erotica," she writes, "if it is to be judged art, should stimulate the fantasy of the onlooker, whereas pornographic inventions leave next to nothing to the imagination."[3]

Pornography (note that we call it pornographic "material") is graphic. It dominates and controls the viewer, leaving no room for his or her individual thoughts and feelings (there aren't a whole lot of interpretive angles that one can take regarding *Debbie Does Dallas*). In essence, pornography reduces people to the status of "things": to quote hard-core film actor Bill, who discusses his acting techniques in Robert Stoller's book *Porn*, "The girl is basically an extension of my left hand."[4]

It's no wonder that when one watches explicit pornographic material for even a little while—probably a half hour will do the trick—one feels empty and numb.

Erotica (note that we call it erotic "art") engenders a dramatically different experience. Consider Luis Buñuel's film *Belle de Jour,* in which Catherine Deneuve plays a housewife whose sexual fantasies tend to domination and submission. Her husband (Jean Sorel) is disinclined to join her in her interests, and so she expresses herself by secretly becoming a prostitute. By relying on possibility-opening gesture rather than possibility-closing explicitness, the film invites the viewer to be curious about his or her own mind. In contrast to the mind-numbing experience of pornography, erotic art such as this leaves one engaged, enlivened, and perhaps a bit jostled out of his or her familiar comfort zones.

The difference between erotica and pornography is not simply, as adult film star Gloria Leonard opined, "the lighting."

Now, using the distinction between erotica and pornography as our frame of reference, let's answer the question with which we began this discussion: What, exactly, is "healthy" sexuality?[5]

At its best, sex is a pleasurable and meaningful way to share important and real aspects of oneself with another who matters. When the independent selfhood of both partners is respectfully preserved in the face of the complex emotions and powerful desires that sex engenders (when difference is recognized and then celebrated), when vulnerability and openness are featured, sex becomes an opportunity for vitality, change, and growth. Healthy sexuality, or, to use the shorthand of this chapter, "real sex," features meaning and connection—the principles of erotica. And it is not characterized by numbness, overstimulation, and control—the principles of pornography.

If we define healthy sexuality in this way, we have a powerful and pragmatic tool for clarifying some of our contemporary confusion regarding sex.

For starters, defining healthy sexuality as a pleasurable and meaningful way to share important aspects of ourselves with another person who matters to us gives us a moralism-free way of thinking about the wide variety of sexual behaviors that we humans engage in. According to this definition, sexual health is not determined by what kind of sex one engages in; straight missionary position sex can be "unhealthy" (or even, to use the technical term, "perverse") when undertaken with the intent of controlling and negating the experience of one's partner. Meanwhile the most unusual sexual practices imaginable can be considered healthy when they are undertaken in an atmosphere of mutual and respectful sharing and play. In other words, sex is "healthy" not according to what it looks like, but according to its meaning and intention.

Moreover, when we think of healthy sexuality as involving respect for the independent selfhood of both partners, it becomes clear that the "hooking up" and "friends with benefits" that many kids talk about are not just a matter of one generation pursuing its mandate to shock the next. When we understand that healthy sexuality features meaning and connection, it becomes obvious that the glossy, disembodied, virtual images of sex that permeate our society are harmful to us. Perhaps these understandings will motivate us to teach our kids that there is an alternative to the kind of sex that is becoming their model, and to speak out against the barrage of sexual overstimulation, in the media and elsewhere, that currently inundates us.

Now let's apply this definition of "healthy sexuality" to our long-term relationships, and to the idea of making our relationships work for us.

At their best our intimate relationships offer us a remarkable opportunity to risk being open and vulnerable with each other. By embracing the way that love can deepen and evolve over time, by recognizing and then celebrating our differences, we teach each other invaluable lessons about who we are. And if we give up our fruitless attempts to try to change our partners, instead opening ourselves to being changed by them, we continue to grow through middle age and beyond.

Sex, in turn, may well be the most direct means by which long-term intimacy can enhance our lives. The immediacy of sexual touch causes us to come together in our deepest, and most vulnerable, places. The unbridled physicality of sex causes us to be momentarily unguarded, even in those areas we are most inclined to protect. And our efforts to make each other feel good cause us to feel cared about in those same vulnerable places.

Real sex, it follows, affords us a nearly unparalleled medium for helping each other to change, grow, and remain alive in both our bodies and our minds.

Dan and Melissa: Sex, Drugs, and Lethal Colds

Over time it became obvious to me that Dan's sexual rituals were a kind of drug, one that he needed in order to feel, as he put it, "marginally OK." This drug had a very specific effect: Dan's compulsive masturbation, his tendency to constantly check his appearance for flaws and blemishes, and his need to conscript Melissa into his sexual rituals—all these and more both masked and reflected complicated feelings that he had about his masculinity.

When I shared my ideas with Dan he didn't reject them, but he didn't exactly embrace them either. "I can't say that you're wrong," he would say, "but I'm not exactly sure where all this gets me."

And at this point we *needed* to get somewhere. As Dan had become more reflective about his relationship with sex, and as our conversations had caused Melissa to become less of a willing partner to his habit, his drug had stopped working, and he was becoming increasingly unhappy.

Then one day, about six months after we had begun to talk with each other, I caught a cold.

Hours of sniffling and coughing had left my voice hoarse and my nose red. Different patients had different reactions, but none were as strong as Dan's. Moving his chair as far away from me as my office would allow, he said, palpably distressed, "Wow, you're really sick. Maybe we should leave."

I apologized, and, perhaps made even denser than usual by the virus, stated the obvious: "You're worried about getting sick."

"Colds are a big deal for Dan," Melissa interjected.

"That's putting it mildly," Dan added. "I hate colds. They make me feel like I'm going to die."

"Die from a cold?" I asked, now quite curious.

For nearly a minute no one said anything. Finally, speaking very softly, I asked: "Where are you?"

"I'm thinking about my father," Dan answered, and with this he began to tell us about a man whom he had barely known, a man who had died when he was ten, and a man who, despite his apparent absence in Dan's life, had dominated his mind for over fifty years.

"My father had bad heart disease," Dan told us. "Whenever I think of him I see him sitting in a wheelchair, wrapped in a blanket, with a nurse sitting next to him. He was all shriveled up, and because he couldn't clear his lungs, he was constantly coughing up this yellow phlegm. He smelled like a nursing home. He was repulsive."

"That's a pretty awful picture of a man getting older," I noted.

"I can't stand the idea of getting old," Dan answered. With these words he violently shook his head, and then, looking up with a wry smile, he said: "You know, this seems so obvious, but it just hit me that the reason I work so hard on my body, the reason I'm so obsessed with sex, is that I'm scared to death of being like my father."

With Dan's hard-won understanding, the nature of his and Melissa's shared struggles became evident.

Probably none of us likes growing old, but for Dan the inevitable bumps and erosions of age felt like a straight line to becoming a sick old man, wrapped in a blanket, sputtering phlegm. Ultimately all of Dan's sexual and bodily compulsions reflected his efforts to deny aging, death, and deterioration by constructing the illusion that he was invincibly masculine. And instead of relating to Melissa as a real person, one who would reflect back to him his imperfect, fallible humanity, he conscripted her into helping him with his denial.

Melissa, in turn, was terrified of being judged. She had made her relationship with Dan into an elaborate shell game, one in which she allowed herself to be Dan's drug while hiding her real self from his criticism. By giving in to Dan's demands she was able to hide her real self behind her compliance.

Together Dan and Melissa had made their sexual relationship into a highly creative means of avoiding both each other and their own deepest fears.

Once the problem had been made clear, the solution also became obvious: Dan and Melissa needed to help each other confront the pain and injury that they had so assiduously avoided. Dan needed to find, through Melissa, a more positive picture of being an older man. And Melissa needed to find, through Dan's acceptance of her, the feeling of being lovable not only to herself but to another.

Of course, this was easier said than done. As Dan said when I shared my ideas with them, "Great. So when are you going to tell us how to actually do it?"

Over the next eighteen months Dan, Melissa, and I worked hard at "actually doing it." My approach, I'll admit, was lacking in art and delicacy, so much so that the couple often joked that I must have received my degree by way of a matchbook advertisement.

I confronted Dan's addiction to pornography, reminding him that the women in the movies he watched weren't actually enjoying what they were doing, and that the men, quite often, felt numb and wooden. I told him that he would never be able to appreciate himself for his significant accomplishments and successes if he could not set the bar more realistically. (Above all, this meant that he would have to accept the fact that he was neither young nor invincible.) And I encouraged him to be real with Melissa, often reminding him that he wouldn't want a man to think of his daughter in the way he thought of his wife.

At the same time I spoke with Melissa about the way that her sexual compliance was an act of self-camouflage. I invoked the couple's daughter; surely Melissa would want her daughter to stand up for herself in future relationships with men, but how would her daughter learn to do so if Melissa herself did not? And, in a maneuver that caused Dan great consternation, I told Melissa not to make love with him unless he first talked with her in an open and honest way: "Hold out on him until he's real with you," I suggested. "He's hiding from you as much as you are from him."

Basically I asked them both to shed their armor—Dan's hyper-masculine illusion of invincibility, and Melissa's bait-and-switch operation—in the service of being real with each other. I encouraged them to face their deepest fears—Dan's fear of death and deterioration, Melissa's fear of not being good enough for someone else. And I tried to sell them on the value of touching each other, really touching each other, in both mind and body.

One day, toward the end of our two years together, I opened the door to my waiting room to greet a laughing Dan and Melissa. As they entered the office I noticed that Dan looked uncharacteristically sheepish. He sat in his chair, broke into a wide grin, and said, "Melissa broke my penis."

"She broke your penis?" I answered, laughing with Dan, but wondering what on earth he was talking about.

Dan and Melissa glanced at each other, and, after an exchange of playful "after yous," she told the story. "Dan and I were making love the other day—actually, we were doing what we usually do before we make love, we were lying in bed talking. Most of the time it feels a little bit like he's trying to be good, like he knows he's not going to get any unless he talks to me first. But this time he was telling me about how hard it was for him to see his dad so sick, and I felt like he really wanted to talk.

"Anyway, there was something about the way he just wanted to be with me, not just for sex, but to actually talk, that made me *want* to have sex with him. So I did something I never do; I started coming on to him. We started fooling around, and then, I couldn't believe it, for the first time in his entire life he couldn't get an erection."

Now Dan picked up the story. "When I couldn't get hard I felt terrible. You know what Melissa does? She doesn't say 'Don't worry, it's OK,' or any of those things women are supposed to say at times like that. No, she says, 'Fuck me you head case.' Excuse me? 'Fuck me you head case'? But you know what? It worked. I got hard right away, she got on top of me, and she was so into it—that's what I meant by 'she broke my penis'—I came in about twenty seconds.

"After it was over we were laughing so hard we couldn't stop. I felt like this huge weight was lifted off my chest. I didn't have to get out of bed and check myself out in the mirror to make sure I was still OK."

"To be frank, the sex kind of sucked," Melissa joined in. "But you know what? I loved it. I felt like I could be myself. Actually, I've felt like I could be myself for a long time now, so it wasn't that. It was that I felt like myself with *him*."

CHOOSE REAL SEX OVER GREAT SEX

Sex can be lots of things.[6, 7] And at different life stages, different meanings may take center stage.

Sex for an adolescent can be about coming to terms with all that is stimulated by entering or being entered. It can be about beginning to deal with anxiety, shame, and guilt. It can be about knowing, and using, one's body. It can be about pleasure, a way to learn, a way to find one's self. Perhaps above all it can be about beginning to put together the overwhelming physical power of sexuality with an ongoing awareness of the "person-hood" of others.

Sex for a young adult looking for a life partner can be about weighing the power and allure of physical attractiveness against the need for honesty, persistence, integrity, sincerity, and other qualities that make relationships work. It can be about finding a partner who will be a good father, or a good mother. It can be a mode of self-expression, a way of communicating intense emotions, hopefully love and affection, but also, at times, contained aggression.

Of course sex can be about creating a family.

And then there is the crucial role of sex in our long-term intimate relationships.

As the years pass, our bodies diverge more and more from the collagen-enhanced, BOTOX-infused, airbrushed images of youth and infinite possibility that have become our ubiquitous cultural ideal. With this divergence we can feel alienated from our lovers, and ourselves. But if we take the risk of being sexually real over time with someone loved and trusted, we will find an alternative to the distorting fun-house mirrors that populate our present-day surroundings. We can, instead, find in each other loving and compassionate reflections of our bodily selves. We can, as did Dan and Melissa, use our sexual relationships to change long-standing, painful, and stagnant scripts. And we can sustain the sense of vibrant physicality that all too easily disappears in the face of life's multiple pressures and, over time, mounting losses.

What can we do, with or without the help of therapy, to build sexual relationships that will help us to grow into our best selves?

- **Fight the airbrushed sexual ideals that have become our cultural currency.** Work on the emotional side of your relationship; our perceptions of attractiveness are mediated by our feelings for each other. The better we feel about each other the better we look to each other.

- **Make a point of being realistic about bodies.** Embrace the changes in your bodies as you age.
- **Get radical about pornography** and the rest of the "It's just sex, it doesn't mean anything" culture that numbs and over-stimulates us. Just avoiding this culture isn't enough; like water in a closed space, it will find all the available cracks. Actively oppose it.
- If you have children, **emphasize the fact that sex is part of a relationship.** That it is best when it is personal. Let your-self appear to be "uncool"; tell them, for example, that it's sexy to leave a little to the imagination.
- **Forget about trying to have "great" sex.** Instead risk being real with each other. Believe in sex that stumbles, that laughs, that makes a point of being human. Make a point of finding each other's eyes.
- **Make a point of having playfully "lousy" sex.**

And if you are the one to take the lead?

- If you aren't having sex, be willing to **acknowledge the problem**, and then **talk about it**.
- **Normalize sex.** Often a major impediment to talking about sex is shame or embarrassment. Make it clear that you un-derstand that what goes on in a person's sexual mind is not to be judged or criticized. Work to create an environment in which anything can be talked about.
- As always, **look at yourself first**. We all have complicated sexualities; it's part of what makes us interesting. Know yourself. Know what you are afraid of, what you avoid,

what makes you feel embarrassed and ashamed. Be willing to take the lead in talking about these things.

- **Bring lightness and humor to your sexual relationship.** Don't let sex get too serious.
- **Be willing to hold on to your own desire even if your partner is sexually withdrawn.** This can be particularly difficult—it isn't easy to want when your partner is unresponsive—but continuing to want under such circumstances can be a powerful way of setting an example.

Above all, **choose "real sex" over "great sex."**

Such Small Things

They lay in bed, lights out after reading, she on her back, he rolled away from her. She was thinking about his socks, the socks that had been on the floor in front of the closet for three days. She had been watching them, hating herself for her small-mindedness, but wondering how long it would take him to pick them up. Grinding under the presumption of servitude, of relative unimportance, she had wondered, as she often did, what it was about her degree, her mind, her time, and her body that he imagined was worth less than his.

And then the socks were gone, and with them her festering annoyance; her brain just let it go. How do such small things help her to feel less angry, to find him again? Sometimes it happened when he looked into her eyes, not by them or through them, into them, like he truly wanted to find her. Sometimes it happened when he opened the refrigerator, grabbed for that third beer (she wondered whether he knew that she counted), but, on seeing her, closed the door and came to bed instead. The big things seemed to mean so little to her—flowers, gifts, protestations of love. But the little things, small moments of caring and noticing—these made all the difference.

With these thoughts she rolled over to him, pressed against his back, and put her arm around him.

He was always surprised when she reached for him in bed. He knew by now her different touches. The "Hello but don't get any ideas" touch. The perfunctory "I haven't touched you for a long time so I'm doing it now" touch. And this touch, the "I can be found if you want me" touch. A gentle rubbing of his stomach, one that didn't stop when he reached back behind him and stroked her thigh. As soon as he knew she would say "yes," the resentment, the building, simmering, weeklong move from longing to grievance let go, melted by her willingness.

Are other women like her, she wondered? She could be so closed to him, his smell, his voice, the weight of his body, his gestures, all could feel so suffocating to her. His need pressed against her, into her, it sucked the air out of the room. But then, with these small moments of noticing and caring, he returned to scale. She could feel her body, her mind, something deeper than both, her self perhaps, not eclipsed by him, but next to him. A warm pressure spread from her breasts to her belly as she lay against his back, and this time she wanted to move toward the feeling in her body, not away from it. The hardening of his penis wasn't exactly exciting, but at least, when it seemed not to be demanding her submission, it could be interesting. The voices still came at her, but she could quiet them.

Thank God, he sighed to himself. The words struck him as odd. Here he was, a forty-five-year-old man thanking God that his wife was willing to make love to him. But grateful was how he felt. Ten years ago he didn't fight the growing sense of grievance in the intervals between sex, he wallowed in feeling cheated. But now he told himself that sex was not a right, it was a gift, and this seemed to help. It helped him, and it seemed to help her.

CHAPTER IV

FIND FREEDOM
THROUGH COMMITMENT

What is freedom? Is it the ability to do whatever one wants whenever one wants? Is it the absence of limit and responsibility?

Ironically, freedom of this sort, if it even exists, is a sure-fire path to loneliness and emptiness. Limitless money? Limitless time? Limitless sex? What is a dollar, a day, or an embrace when the next one might be more or better? No, we won't find meaning and happiness by trying to transcend the universal constraints that govern and organize our lives; we'll find it by respecting them.

Real freedom, it follows, won't come from replacing reality with daydreams. It will come from harnessing our strengths and talents (and even those same daydreams) so that we can live fully and well within the world as it is.

Our long-term intimate relationships can be a terrific medium for learning to respect those realities we cannot change,[1] and for learning how such respect can help us to live more meaningful and vibrant lives. And there is no single aspect of those relationships that better teaches us this lesson than commitment.

Find freedom through commitment. This is the fourth resolution.

So what do we mean when we talk about "commitment" in an intimate relationship? For most of us the word conjures notions of sexual fidelity, which is certainly an important expression of loyalty and faithfulness. But eschewing promiscuity is only one manifestation of commitment, one that does not by itself guarantee a good relationship. Many of us who have never had an affair emotionally abandoned our spouses years ago, while some of us who have had affairs have built and sustained deeply committed and meaningful relationships.

No, the kind of commitment that makes intimate relationships thrive is more encompassing than the relatively straightforward matter of whether or not one strays sexually. Among its many qualities, commitment involves the willingness to stay true when things get tough. It requires grappling with hard and painful parts of oneself in order to remain real and present. And it means investing the time and effort necessary to create a shared and private space in which the creative friction of long-term intimacy can change both partners.

Commitment, at its best, is not an outdated convention, a moralistic edict aimed at suppressing sexuality and individuality. It is a radical, personal choice that allows us to risk exploring, with a trusted other, the most hidden and most vulnerable corners of our selves.

ETHAN AND OLIVIA

When Ethan Gilbert first contacted me, he told me that he and his wife Olivia were looking for "a little sex therapy." I told Ethan that I would be glad to talk with them, but, caveat emptor, I wasn't exactly a sex therapist.

"We know," Ethan responded. "We got a sense of what you do from a friend who gave us your name. I'm pulling your leg a bit—we don't really need an actual sex therapist, but we do need to talk with someone about sex."

"Talking about sex is certainly up my alley," I answered, sensing Ethan's playfulness. "Let's find a time."

Ethan and Olivia were a delightfully lively couple in their early sixties. Ethan, an only child, was a bit on the gnomish side, balding and short, but his bright and engaging eyes gave him a certain charisma. Olivia, the oldest of four daughters, was an elegant gray-haired woman who was at least two inches taller than her husband. Though different in their looks they seemed a good fit: they were clearly fond of each other; they exuded energy about their careers as university professors (Ethan's expertise lay in Middle Eastern studies, Olivia's in art history); and they clearly enjoyed their three children and, in a new development, two grandchildren.

"So what's on your minds about sex?" I asked, soon after the start of our first session. I was trying to recapture the playful tone of the initial phone conversation, but, I'll confess, I felt like a bull in a china shop.

Ethan and Olivia looked shyly at each other, and then Ethan took the lead.

"We've had a very good sexual life over the years," he began, speaking with more propriety and less playfulness than he had over the phone. "Then five years ago Olivia had a mastectomy. The prognosis was good then, and it's even better now that the time has passed cancer-free. But our sexual life has never been the same. I don't really think it's me. I've always loved being with Olivia sexually, and I still do. But she's having trouble feeling comfortable again."

Ethan paused, and we both looked expectantly at Olivia.

"This really isn't about Ethan," Olivia began, speaking directly, comfortably, and less formally than her husband. "I wanted to talk to someone myself, but he pointed out that sex is something we do together [here the couple shared a brief, light laugh]. When we first got involved he helped me a lot with sex.

But since my mastectomy I feel terrible about my body, and I can't seem to get over it."

Ethan and Olivia had clearly lost a great deal since the surgery. Not only did they rarely make love—perhaps five or six times over the past five years—they now slept on opposite sides of the bed, they rarely touched, and they had grown short and impatient with each other. What was worse, they had lost, at least for the time being, a special bond: "We've always considered ourselves each other's best friends," Ethan said. "I guess that's still true, but we don't often feel like best friends anymore."

We began by talking about what had happened in the wake of Olivia's illness. The conversation was intimate and fascinating, revolving as it did around her feelings about the surgery, her doubts that Ethan could find her desirable, and the way her sense of herself as a woman had changed. Ethan and Olivia weren't so sure, however, that these were the topics that they needed to talk about. They had been able to have these discussions on their own, they noted, and they wondered whether deeper issues that they couldn't articulate might be in the way.

Sure enough, our conversations soon gave way to a darker subtext.

"I realized this odd thing about my cancer," Olivia observed, perhaps four months into our work together. "There are survivor groups, chat rooms, forums of all kinds for people who want to talk about their illness and their treatments. But I have absolutely no interest in talking to anybody. It's not because I'm shy—I was pretty shy when we first got married, but I grew out of that years ago. And it isn't because of my 'denial' either; I was able to face the *fact* that I had cancer, even the possibility of my own death. What's hard is that I feel it's my dirty little secret. I feel ashamed of having had cancer."

"Why do you feel ashamed?" I asked.

"I suspect that it has something to do with this thing that happened a long time ago with my uncle," Olivia answered. Then, after a moment's pause, she added: "At least the feelings are awfully similar."

Olivia told us the story, which was old news for Ethan but a revelation to me. When she was thirteen an uncle had fondled her breasts on several occasions, an experience that had left her with a great deal of anxiety around sex, a feeling that her body was ugly and dirty, and a deep sense of shame. She had told Ethan about what had happened early in their relationship, and she had found his outrage at her uncle, along with his kindness toward her, reassuring and even reparative.

"Early on we would often just lie in bed holding each other," she said. "If I didn't feel like making love that was OK with him. And then when we did have sex—what was that Marvin Gaye song? 'Sexual Healing'? That's what it used to feel like."

Now, however, Olivia's shame had returned. Was it possible that her illness and the surgery had dredged up old feelings related to the molestation?

Olivia, Ethan, and I spent the next several weeks talking about the abuse that she had endured.

"Did I tell you that my uncle told me that what he did to me was *my* idea?" Olivia asked. "That he promised not to tell anyone because *I* would get in trouble? He said we could make it our secret."

"Bastard," I heard Ethan mutter under his breath.

"He *was* a bastard," Olivia said. "But I think we're figuring something out here. It seems pretty clear that I feel the same shame about my cancer."

As do most kids who are sexually abused, Olivia had felt as if she were to blame for what had happened to her. What was more, again as do most children who are sexually abused, Olivia had had enormously confusing feelings of physiological arousal during the molestation. This wasn't a reflection of her "wanting it," as her uncle had told her, it was the inevitable consequence of her body reacting normally to physical stimulation even in the face of a highly abnormal situation. These feelings, along with her uncle's propaganda, formed the core of her shame and guilt.

With this understanding Olivia, Ethan, and I had found our way to a critical truth. Present-day injury—Olivia's cancer—had interacted with an old trauma—her abuse—to create a perfect storm of trouble: cancer and the subsequent surgery had once again placed a painful and unwanted focus on Olivia's breasts, bringing up decades-dormant feelings of shame and guilt.

"I just remembered that I had the strangest thought when I was being wheeled into the surgery," Olivia told us, midway through one of our more intense conversations. "It wasn't clear whether or not I would need a mastectomy—they were going to do the biopsy and make the decision while I was still anesthetized—but somehow I knew I was going to wake up without my breast. And I thought: 'this is what I deserve.' At the time I figured it was just the drugs taking over, but now I get it. It was that old feeling that I deserved to be punished for what I did back then coming out."

Revisiting, and Then Reworking, an "Old, Bad Pattern"

The recognition that Olivia was once again awash in shame and guilt had helped Ethan and Olivia to feel less short and impatient with each other, but it didn't bring them the result they most wanted: to find their way back to each other in bed.

Olivia had an idea about why things still felt stuck sexually:

"I think that we've talked about the piece of this that's mine," she said, "and now it feels like there's something we both need to work on."

I wondered what she had in mind.

"I think we've gotten into some old patterns," Olivia answered. "Some old, bad patterns."

With these words Ethan and Olivia began to tell me about a problem that they had encountered years before. It's a problem that most, if not all, couples have to solve, and it's one that, when we fail to solve it, easily leads to distance and resentment: the sticky business of who gets to feel like the more important person in the relationship, and who has to take a backseat.

Early on, when Olivia was still struggling with fallout from her uncle's abuse, she had been shy about drawing attention to herself. Ethan, on the other hand, had been very willing to take up space, both in the relationship and in his life at large. "He may be a small man physically," Olivia noted, "but everybody is aware of Ethan when he walks into the room. I was pretty scared when we were younger, and while I hate to admit it, back then it probably worked for me to let him be the big cheese."

As the couple entered their forties, as their three children began to get older, and as Olivia returned to full-time work, this arrangement became less functional. Olivia, now largely free from the shame and guilt that had strangled her when she first married, began to bristle under the presumption of Ethan's relative importance. Ethan, in turn, began to find Olivia's passivity frustrating; he wished that she would assert herself more, both in her life and in their relationship.

Fortunately, Ethan and Olivia were able to change this "old, bad pattern."

Ethan recognized that he was crowding Olivia out of the relationship, and he vowed to be less self-centered. "I had no idea that I was part of the problem until she pointed out to me that I could be terribly self-centered," he admitted, speaking in his familiarly erudite manner. "But I learned from Olivia that I wasn't always the most important person in the room, or, for that matter, in the relationship."

Olivia, meanwhile, vowed to assert herself more, both in the relationship and in her life at large. "We *both* worked at it," she recalled. "I remember a time when we both had job interviews on the same day. I came home, Ethan asked me how it went, and I said: 'I pretended I was you—I told them how great I was.' And Ethan said, 'That's hilarious. I was worried about my reputation for being arrogant, so *I* pretended I was *you*. I made sure I didn't spend the whole interview telling them how great I was.'"

"But I think we're back there again," Olivia continued. "Maybe because you had to take care of me when I was sick, maybe because I've felt some of that old shame that made me want to hide, maybe because I had to stop working for a while, whatever the reason, the assumption that you're more important than me feels like it's back.

Ethan and Olivia knew what they had to do: Ethan would have to once again cede some space and some control, Olivia would have to once again live a little larger, and together the couple would have to rebalance themselves.

Sounds easy, at least in the abstract. Unfortunately, real-life changes tend to be more difficult than this. If we are going to reverse old, problematic habits and behaviors, we usually have to confront, and tolerate, the same painful feelings that caused us to get off track in the first place.

This was certainly the case for Ethan and Olivia. Ethan tended to get "a little controlling" when he was scared, and he was terrified that his beloved wife was going to die. Olivia tended to hide behind Ethan's formidable presence when she felt ashamed, and the recent assault on her breasts had made her feel very ashamed.

If we were going to change things, therefore, we would have to take some of the sting out of Ethan's fear and Olivia's shame, and so lighten their dependence on their primary ways of managing distress: his control and her withdrawal.

I suspect that Ethan and Olivia's solution will sound to you like an incredibly difficult undertaking. It was. But what they did is also, in its essence, a model for what we *all* have to do if we are to change our relationships and our selves: they tied themselves in, they talked openly and honestly about their deepest fears and vulnerabilities, and they treated those fears and vulnerabilities with care and kindness.

In Ethan and Olivia's case the talking took the form of a kind of game.

The rules of the game were simple; they agreed to take off their clothes, get in bed, hold each other, and talk to each other about what most pained them. Olivia's part was to talk to Ethan about her cancer, her body, her uncle, and her shame. Ethan's part was to talk to Olivia about his fear that he would lose her. And both had to stay as emotionally present as possible.

Ethan began by telling Olivia how he really felt about her body. "I've been saying in here that I still love her body, and that's mostly true. But over the last few weeks, while we've been playing this game—we call it 'the crying game' because that's all we do, cry—I've been realizing that I haven't let myself know the whole truth. I look at Olivia's scar and I turn away. I touch it and I feel horrified."

"To be perfectly honest, I *do* miss her breast," he continued. "But it's not the changes in her body itself that I can't stand. What's unbearable is what her illness signifies: her mortality. Whenever I look at the scar, whenever I touch it, I have to force myself not to turn away because the eventuality of her death feels so real."

Over time, as Ethan forced himself to talk with Olivia about these feelings, he began to replace his terror with a sense of calm. What happened wasn't magic: even the most unbearable feelings can be made bearable when we face them in the company of someone whom we love, and who loves us. And in Ethan and Olivia's case, making painful feelings more bearable proved enormously helpful.

"I knew, on some level, that Ethan wasn't telling me the whole truth; I could *feel* that he couldn't stand to look at me. The problem wasn't that he couldn't look, though; it was *why* I thought he couldn't look. I didn't know that he was scared of losing me, I figured he was disgusted by me. And I took that right to 'I'm a disgusting person because of what I did with my uncle.' Yeah, I know my uncle was the bad guy, but that's my rational adult mind. There will always be a little-girl part of me that still feels like what happened was my fault, and that I *should* be really ashamed.

"You know how you've been telling us to talk to that little-girl part of me?" (I had indeed been asking Ethan and Olivia, as part of their "game," to speak directly to those closeted-off parts of Olivia that still held the shame of her abuse.) "You know how I give you a hard time for sounding so 'New-Agey'? Well, we've been telling that little-girl part that it wasn't her fault. And I think it's making me feel better."

As Ethan and Olivia continued to play together, seriously and creatively, Olivia's shame began to lift.

As Ethan felt like he had her back, his fear of losing her began to recede.

With these changes they were able to create a very real and very grounded kind of freedom: to repeat a central theme, they couldn't change many of the hard realities that had impacted their lives—the abuse, the cancer, and the fact of their aging. But by being fully themselves with each other they could soften the impact of those realities, transforming them from life-crushing traumas to life-shaping, human hardships.

MEN AND WOMEN CHANGING TOGETHER
THROUGH THEIR COMMITMENTS

As Ethan and Olivia show us, we don't live fully by trying to avoid life's hardships. Rather we do so by finding the courage to learn from life's challenges. In Ethan and Olivia's case these challenges included not only Olivia's cancer, but also one of the most common problems faced in heterosexual relationships: that of relative power and importance.

In exploring their solution we can learn a great deal about how men and women, when they are open to being changed by one another, can learn from each other's differences. We may have to enter some politically dicey territory to do so, but I believe that it will be worth our while.

As relationships deepen, couples develop shared perspectives, shared sets of values, and shared identities.[2] A "we" develops alongside a "you" and a "me," and intimate partners come to resemble each other in speech patterns, stylistic preferences, and, amazingly enough, appearance. Over time men and women even approach each other across the sometimes vast divide of gender; when a man is open to being changed by a woman he can become more open to his feminine qualities, while a woman, similarly, can become more open to her masculine side.

What do we mean when we speak of masculine and feminine "qualities"? To be sure, these words have many meanings, but one essential dimension, the one most relevant to Ethan and Olivia's story, is illuminated by the contemporary research on parenting.

Careful observation of interactions between fathers, mothers, and infants[3] tells us that mothers tend to closely and accurately tune in to their children. They then reflect their children's experience back in ways that allow those children to see, feel, and know their own selves through the mirror of their mother's reactions.

Fathers, on the other hand, play in a much more stimulating, vigorous, and arousing manner. If mothers tend to fold themselves into their children, then fathers disrupt, and in doing so they tend to take up a great deal more space.

Taken together, these characteristic ways of relating offer children an invaluable balance between two fundamental childhood lessons: the softness of "the world can be your oyster" and the hardness of "the world is a tough place, and you'll have to learn to deal with it."

Early in their relationship these differences could be seen in Ethan and Olivia; he was a real take-up-space kind of man, and she, at that time, was anything but a take-up-space kind of woman. Once again, this arrangement worked well for a while, but then it began to unravel: "I started to feel like I was suffocating," Olivia remembered. "The turning point was when Ethan traveled to London for a week to lecture, and all of a sudden I could feel myself. That was when I realized how much I'd been disappearing into him. It wasn't his fault and it wasn't mine, it was just the way we fit together back then."

Fortunately Ethan and Olivia had two central truths working in their favor, truths that tend to be overlooked in the often-incendiary debates about gender. First, the differences between men and women are relative and not absolute.[4,5] Second, the differences between men and women are negotiable.[6] (The same research that shows observable differences between fathers and mothers also shows that single mothers tend to become more "paternal" in their style, while single fathers move to more "maternal" positions.)

These truths gave Ethan and Olivia the flexibility to change themselves, and so to change their relationship. Ethan became more receptive; he learned that he could surrender without having to submit. Olivia became more assertive; she learned to be more forceful and to take up more space. And together the couple found a less polarized and more rewarding way to "fit together."

How did they do this? Once again, they struggled things out together. They played with each other. And above all, they influenced each other (recall the interviews in which Ethan pretended that he was Olivia, and Olivia pretended that she was Ethan). Because the "we" of the relationship mattered as much to them as did the "I" of their individual selves, they were open to being changed by each other, and so they were able to grow into what had been dormant parts of themselves.

That men can learn from women, and women from men, may be a common and important way that we change each other,[7] but it is by no means the only way that we strengthen ourselves through our long-term commitments. By staying with their relationship Jason and Leslie were able to remember how much they cared about each other, and in doing so they found their way back to their compassion and their shared values. By recapturing their sexuality Michael and Susan were able to remain alive and vital in both their minds and their bodies. By helping each other to tolerate the pain of their early losses Noah and Devon were able to risk loving each other more deeply. And by helping Dan to remember his sickly father Melissa made it possible for him to appreciate himself as a successful, healthy, albeit older, man.

These relationships all illustrate a critical truth, one that is easily overlooked in our "me-first" culture: when we remain faithful and committed to each other over time, when we put the "we" of a relationship before the "I" of our individual selves, we don't diminish those individual selves, we strengthen them.

Monogamy: An "Intimate Exploration into One Other Person"[8]

During the course of our conversations Ethan and Olivia told me about a difficult time that had occurred some two years after Olivia's surgery. This aspect of their story never seemed particularly central to them—we probably spent no more than an hour or two on it—but it stayed with me. At the height of Ethan and Olivia's post-surgery unhappiness Ethan had engaged in, as he put it, "the only blemish in my otherwise long and faithful husbandly career."

"I guess it was my midlife crisis," Ethan admitted. "I was frustrated with how unhappy and distant Olivia was. If I'm perfectly honest with myself, I was probably also unhappy being an aging, balding academic. I bought the sports car, but that didn't seem to do the trick, so I got myself in a spot of trouble."

Ethan began a flirtation with a younger professor at his university, a woman in her mid-forties who had told him that she had a crush on him. Over several months Ethan and the younger professor spent quite a bit of time talking. The relationship progressed as far as a little hand-holding, and then talk of having sex.

"I was in a trance," Ethan told us, "but when we actually talked about going to bed I was shocked out of it. I told Olivia right away. At first she was terribly upset, but we talked late into the night, and eventually she became incredibly understanding. I spoke to the woman the next day and ended it, and I've never looked back. But it was a closer call than I'd like to admit."

That Ethan chose fidelity meant the world to Olivia. "If he had consummated that relationship," she said, ever dignified but always direct, "I doubt that I could have trusted him again. I know that sounds old-fashioned, but I don't primarily mean it in a moral sense. For me being faithful means that we have something that is different from what we have with anyone else. I believe what Ethan says to me about how he feels about me. What he says to me about my body. I believe in the privacy of our bedroom. I'm not talking just about sex, I'm talking about something deeper. The fact that Ethan is faithful to me is what makes it possible for me to let him into the places where all that messed-up stuff with my uncle lives, into all the other places in me that feel dark and ugly. If he'd slept with that woman I'd have felt like I was letting her in too."

How important is sexual fidelity to a long-term intimate relationship?

Over the years biologists have marveled over certain animals that appear to be models of monogamy. A case in point is the prairie vole, a furry little creature that has recently received a great deal of press for its supposed lifelong fidelity. Well, it turns out that prairie voles aren't exactly the paragons of faithfulness that they were once thought to be;[9] there are, in fact, very few models of monogamy in the natural world.

And we humans are no exception, although it's hard to tell from the available statistics just how wanton we are. As Tom Smith of the University of Chicago notes, "There are probably more scientifically worthless 'facts' on extra-marital relations than on any other facet of human behavior."[10] While popular magazines like *Redbook* and *Cosmopolitan*, advice columnists like Dear Abby and Dr. Joyce Brothers, and "pop-sexologists" like Shere Hite all report "studies" that show extremely high levels of extramarital sexual activity (Peggy Vaughan, author of *The Monogamy Myth*,[11] suggests that a conservative estimate is that 60 percent of men and 40 percent of women will have an extramarital affair), more rigorous scientific surveys tend to suggest lower levels of infidelity. Indeed, some studies indicate that as few as 15 to 17 percent of married people have affairs.

The actual rates of infidelity may indeed be lower than the

advice gurus, the media, and even a nonscientific perusal of behaviors among our peer groups might lead us to believe, but
there is little doubt that many of us find remaining sexually
faithful and committed a struggle. It's a rare day in my office
that I don't speak with someone who is considering an affair,
having an affair, or dealing with the consequences of having
had an affair. And affairs certainly are a common fixture on the
landscape of midlife: how often do both men and women try to
ease the pain of aging, sexual disinterest, feeling less attractive,
loss, and limitation by finding temporary solace in the arms of
another? As one middle-aged man said to me about his affair
with his twenty-year-younger secretary, "I knew it was a bad
idea every step of the way, but I just couldn't stand the idea that
my wife was the last woman I was ever going to screw."

So is an affair (or two) really such a big deal, particularly
in this "It's-just-sex-it-doesn't-mean-anything-anyway" age? Is
monogamy a necessary, nonnegotiable component of a good
relationship?

Certainly sexual fidelity is not the sine qua non of a good
relationship. I've known countless couples who have never considered an affair whose marriages are either stagnant or filled
with acrimony, and I've worked with many couples who have
found their way back to stronger and more meaningful relationships after one, in many ways because they have been willing
to sort out the inevitable post-affair carnage (Jason and Leslie
being a prime example).

What's more, there are many ways that one can be unfaithful
without actually having sex outside of the marriage. Emotional
connections that supplant the closeness of one's relationship,
that are secret, and that would be hurtful to one's partner if he
or she knew of them are all betrayals, and therefore are, in a
very real sense, acts of infidelity.

To judge an intimate relationship solely on the yes-no basis of whether one has an affair would be absurd. Faithfulness and commitment are not only determined by sexual monogamy, they grow out of an enduring willingness to be present, real, and vulnerable, to make sacrifices, to put "we" before "I," and to struggle with those parts of one's self that get in the way of loving and being loved.

At the same time, as Olivia would have us know, an affair *is* a big deal.

Continued growth and aliveness depend on the construction and preservation of an intensely private, deeply engaged, and unassailably safe intimate space. Sexual fidelity, when it comes from free choice rather than moralistic constraint, and when it is accompanied by openness, vulnerability, and the willingness to take intimate risks, can be a powerful component of such a space. This is particularly true today, as the illusory promise of great and never-ending sex has become the epitome of our society's quest for the unlimited possible. Within this context monogamy can serve as a powerful communication of a couple's choice to forego individual gratifications of the moment in order to find deeper and more enduring meaning together.

Perhaps Holly Brubach captures it best, when, in reviewing the work of the author Ian McEwan, she writes: "[monogamy] is the intimate investigation into one other person as a means to enlarge our experience of the world."[12]

Why Serial Monogamy Won't Work

If we are changed by our openness to new experience, wouldn't a never-ending stream of new lovers, and hence a never-ending stream of novel experience, lead to unlimited personal growth? The answer to this question is that it wouldn't, and the reasons for this answer illuminate why the resolution to be faithful and committed can expand, rather than limit, real freedom.

To begin with, there is that pesky matter of time. If we were to fall in love again and again, simply moving on at the moment that infatuation began to fade, we would spend our days immersed in the timelessness of romantic passion. Sounds great, doesn't it? Well, it certainly seems as if it would feel good to live forever in the omnipotent feeling of having stopped the relentless progression of time, but in fact living in this illusion would eventually lead to emptiness and boredom.

Impermanence, the painful consequence of time's passage, gives our lives meaning.[13] As Adam Phillips writes: "Death makes life lovable; it is the passing of things that is the source of our happiness."[14] Or, to put it in a slightly more hip way, as Joni Mitchell says, "You don't know what you got 'til it's gone."

Then there is the matter of choice and its centrality to a well-lived life. If we were allowed to move from new lover to new lover at the slightest whim,[15] if we could be reassured that all of our disappointments could be cured by finding someone new and even more perfect, we would never learn a critical life lesson: we simply can't have it all. All meaningful choices involve both the realization of potential gain and also the acceptance of inevitable loss. If we were able to choose partner after partner we would, paradoxically, never know the kind of real freedom that comes from harnessing our own capacities, and then using those capacities to make choices that allow us to live the best lives we possibly can.

Finally, there is the matter of how we grow from colliding with our lovers' authentic and separate selves. If we were to repeatedly fall in love we would constantly see our lovers (and ourselves) through the rosy, dopamine-hued glow of romance. It might be extraordinarily pleasurable to spend our lives falling back into love again and again, each time finding in our partners reflected idealized images of ourselves, but we would never benefit from the transformative friction that comes from intimately knowing, and being intimately known by, someone different and separate from ourselves. We would never achieve the kind of love Iris Murdoch refers to when she writes: "Love...is the extremely difficult realization that something other than oneself is real."

No, serial monogamy might be fun for a while, but like a bad dream of drinking water that never quenches one's thirst, it would ultimately plunge us into an ever-deepening well of emptiness. Real freedom, once again, comes not from living a life lacking in constraint, but from freeing ourselves from the constraints that occur when we cannot tolerate aspects of our own being. True liberation, it follows, comes from the kind of self-acceptance that we find when we commit ourselves to our long-term intimate relationships.

PLANNING YOUR INTIMATE TRAVELS

Many of us fantasize about traveling when we retire. We dream of seeing worlds we have never seen, of expanding our horizons after a lifetime of working and responsibly launching our families. What if we consider a different kind of travel? What if we consider exploring not only the faraway lands that we have always longed to see, but also the endlessly fascinating landscape of our own, and of our partner's, inner selves?

Here are a few guidelines for the ambitious, but achievable, goal of finding a world of possibility in the intimate space of a committed, long-term relationship.

- **If you are considering an affair, ask yourself some hard questions.** What haven't you been willing to talk about with your partner? And what parts of yourself are you protecting by not talking about these things? More often than not, an affair is the safer path; a means of avoiding deeper, more meaningful, and often more risky intimacy. It is a way not of moving toward something better, but of moving away from something harder.

- **Be honest with yourself.** If you find yourself saying: "I can be myself with him/her in ways that I can't with my husband/wife," ask why this seems so. Sometimes your partner *will* have trouble with ways that you are. But if these ways really matter to you, have the courage to persevere.
- **Focus on the gains, and not the costs, of commitment.** Yes, commitment does involve sacrifice. So does everything that is worthwhile. But when it comes to intimate commitment, the upside far outweighs the down.
- **Invest.** The kind of commitment that enables us to change and grow requires effort. We all want to retreat; we all have to force ourselves to be open, particularly when things are stormy. When it comes to our intimate relationships, we get back what we put in.
- **Remind yourself that real freedom won't come from transcending constraint;** rather it will come from harnessing your strengths and talents so that you can live fully and well within the world as it is.

Commitment in an intimate relationship is, almost by definition, a shared endeavor. Therefore it is hard to commit when you feel your partner is unwilling to do so to the same degree. What's more, it can be a daunting task to try to encourage your partner to raise his or her level of commitment. But it's not impossible. The key is that somewhat-hard-to-pin-down-but-ultimately-quite-powerful tool that shows up again and again in these passages of advice for those who must, relatively speaking, take on the lion's share of the relationship burden—modeling:

- **Don't focus on what you think your partner is doing wrong.** Instead ask yourself what contribution you are making to the troubles.
- **Emphasize "we" over "I."** Be more concerned with what you can give to the relationship than about what you can get from your partner.
- **Think and talk about commitment in positive terms.** These days commitment can legitimately be considered a radical, even "cool," choice, not a conventional one.
- Above all, **model commitment.** And don't be self-righteous about it.

The Hug at the Door

"That was quite a hug Chuck gave you on the way out," Jesse said, immediately regretting the way that his irritation showed.

"Chuck can be pretty familiar," Amy answered, her tone more factual than her husband's. "Especially when he's had a few glasses of wine."

"'Familiar'? Familiar as in basically grabbing your ass?" Jesse slid the key into the car's ignition with a little extra emphasis. "Not that you seemed to mind."

"Jealous?" Amy's voice turned playful; she was trying to keep things light.

Jesse thought back on the party. Probably he didn't have much right to complain. After all, he'd spent most of the evening imagining what the wives' bodies looked like beneath the carefully chosen clothing of well-to-do middle age.

Amy, too, thought back on the evening. She hadn't liked having Chuck's hand—really it had been more on her hip than on her ass. She hadn't liked it because she didn't much like Chuck. But now, in the comfort of the car ride home, she realized that the hug had caused her another quieter, and surprisingly unfamiliar, feeling. She had felt desired.

Jesse broke the silence. "So do you find Chuck attractive?"

"Puhllease, are you kidding?" Now Amy was fighting hard to steer Jesse away from a serious talk; she didn't want to lose the private pleasure of feeling attractive to the shared space of their conversation.

"Do *you*?" she asked, turning the focus back to Jesse.

"Do I what? Do I find Chuck attractive?"

"No, jerk. Do you find *other women* attractive?"

Jesse lightened. There were no great secrets here; of course he noticed other women, and of course she knew that he noticed. But talking out loud about how much he looked was a level of real that he had never put on the table.

"C'mon," Amy pressed. "I know you look. Talk to me about sex. Tell me what you really think about." She surprised herself. Maybe it was the wine, maybe she was emboldened by feeling desirable, but now she wanted to invite her husband toward the same place that she had just decoyed him away from.

Jesse had heard his wife's question, but by now he had moved on from thinking about other women to an odd feeling that he'd had when he saw his friend embrace his wife. It was the same odd feeling that he had felt in the dreams he'd been having lately, dreams in which Amy was attracted to other men. She never actually had sex with them, but she wanted them in the same hungry way that she had once wanted him. The oddness was that instead of feeling jealous in the dreams, he loved her in a more raw and immediate way than the shifting mix of comfort and disappointment that they had now.

They sat in the car in silence, Amy's exhortation to talk still hanging in the air. Finally Jesse returned to her question.

"Yeah, I think about women all the time. All the time."

"I'm glad to hear that," she said.

The ease in her voice surprised him. "You're *glad* to hear that?" he asked.

"I'm *really* glad to hear that. I've been thinking about something lately. Have you noticed how the more trustworthy things get the more boring they get?"

"Isn't that the compromise they say we all have to make?" Jesse asked, a note of condescension in his voice. "That marriage means trading in excitement for safety, or something like that?" Jesse was annoyed with his own reasonableness. Tonight the usual agreement to keep things safe seemed to have been suspended, and he was again hiding behind that damned rationality of his.

Amy rescued them from the impending safety: "It seems like trusting each other should make it *easier* to talk about hard stuff."

Amy's encouragement propelled Jesse back toward the conversation. "So be honest," he said. "Do you really have no interest in having sex with Chuck?"

"I really have no interest in screwing or being screwed by Chuck," Amy answered emphatically. "But, being honest now, I did like it that he wanted me."

"Isn't the fact that I want you enough?"

"I'm not so sure you do want me, Jesse," Amy said softly.

"Are you serious? I'm the one who's always wishing we had more sex, not you."

"You want sex, but that doesn't necessarily mean that you want *me*."

Jesse forced himself to stay with the truth his wife had spoken. He thought about how he closed his eyes these days when they made love. He closed them because the very things that used to excite him—her voice, her smell, the realness of her body—now felt like intrusions. But when he'd seen Chuck embrace her he'd felt the same feeling he'd felt in his dreams. He had wanted her. Not just sex, her.

"So lately I've been having these dreams," he began.

PART TWO

SHARED
CHOICES

The first four resolutions described in this book,

- **Embrace a longer-lasting vision of love**
- **Celebrate your differences**
- **Have real sex**
- **Find liberation through commitment**

lay the foundation for keeping our relationships vital and alive during the many conflicts, many hardships, and many changes of long-lasting intimacy. These resolutions guide us in our efforts to build a safe space in which we can risk being open with each other in minds, selves, and bodies.

From this point forward the resolutions described in this book undergo a subtle shift. The four that remain,

- **Believe in something more important than yourselves**
- **Give up your habits and addictions**
- **Forgive and give thanks**
- **Play**

also aid us in our efforts to build and sustain a long-term relationship. Their relative emphasis, however, is more on personal growth than on relationship building. These latter resolutions show us how the creative friction of long-term intimacy can expand our experience of ourselves and of our world.

Taken together, all eight resolutions answer the question "why stay together?" in an emphatically positive way: "Because our long-term intimate relationships can help us to become our best selves."

HAPTER V

BELIEVE IN SOMETHING MORE IMPORTANT THAN YOURSELVES[1]

At its core, this book relies on a simple paradox: the best way to strengthen our *individual selves* is to be open to *others* who matter.

Unfortunately, our present-day tendency toward myopic self-interest can cause us to neglect this important truth. Often, it follows, we try to nurture our selves in precisely the wrong ways.

Clara and Austin asked me to help them stop fighting. Their request was an understandable one; their arguments got pretty nasty. Clara frequently screamed at Austin, often in front of their kids, calling him "wimpy," "effete," and "soft." Austin never really lost his temper, but when he spoke to Clara in a coldly critical tone, calling her "unintelligent," "sloppy," and "unsophisticated," his words were no less hurtful.

At first I tried to sell Clara and Austin on the idea that their fights might express old wounds and unacknowledged needs, and I argued that opening up about those wounds and needs might take some of the sting out of them. The couple wasn't buying: "We have pretty much a perfect life except for the arguments," Clara said. "We don't really care *why* we do it, we just want to *stop doing it*."

On the surface Clara and Austin did have something of a "perfect" life. Both had successful careers, they drove expensive cars, they had a lovely house in a prestigious neighborhood, and they gave their two young children all the advantages of lessons, camps, and private schools. Family money had recently allowed them to buy a second house on Martha's Vineyard, and they were quite strategic about involving themselves in the best social circles. They appeared to do everything right; except, of course, for the fact that they were tearing each other to shreds every night.

Oh, and one more thing: their lives, while shiny and successful, seemed utterly joyless.

For eight months we worked according to Clara and Austin's rules. I learned not to ask them *why* they were hurting each other, and after a few futile forays I also stopped asking them about how empty their lives seemed. Talking about why they never made love was certainly off-limits. Instead I took the workmanlike approach of teaching Clara and Austin to recognize the key words that set off the arguments, to call time-outs when the fights did start, and to apologize in the aftermath.

For the most part Clara and Austin were dutiful students, and things got much better.

Eight months after we had begun, Clara and Austin thanked me politely, ending our work. For several years I continued to think of them, always with a degree of uneasiness. I didn't understand what troubled me until I began to write this chapter.

I suppose that on some level Clara and Austin cared about each other, but I never felt that they loved each other very deeply. They were certainly driven to be successful, but it didn't seem to me that they believed in their work. They were conscientious parents, at least to a degree, but even with their kids it seemed that they lacked a level of feeling and commitment. Perhaps I am being unfair, but in retrospect the words of T. S.

Eliot seemed to apply: "There is no greater treason than to do the right thing for the wrong reason." Clara and Austin didn't want to stop fighting because they felt badly about hurting each other, or even because their arguments created a lousy environment for their children. They wanted to stop fighting because not fighting was the final item on their perfect-life checklist.

In chapter II, I wrote about how we try to keep ourselves safe in our intimate relationships by making our partners into familiar and controlled "habits," thus sparing ourselves the risk of encountering their separate and unpredictable selves. By doing this we deprive ourselves of meaningful interaction with real and separate others, and so we undermine our relationships, and our own growth.

Just as we grow by treating our lovers as real and independent beings, thus allowing them to really matter to us, so do we grow when we give up our omnipotence and control in order to allow life itself to really matter.

"Allow life itself to really matter"? Doesn't life already matter to virtually all of us? Sure, but growing older requires a subtle but important shift in our relationship with *how* it matters. Returning to a now-familiar theme, monogamy makes sex meaningful. Struggle makes achievement meaningful. Financial limitation makes money meaningful. And on perhaps the deepest level of all, the finite nature of time makes the time that we have left meaningful. Allowing life to matter requires that we do what Clara and Austin could not: that we let go, radically and completely, of the illusion of perfectibility, and that we instead embrace the notion that life reveals its joys and meanings through its limitations.

Believe in something more important than yourselves. This is the fifth resolution. When we believe in something more important than ourselves we see ourselves in scale, we open ourselves to learning from a world that has much to teach us, and we grow into our less self-centered, and therefore better, selves.

Our long-term, intimate relationships offer us a terrific forum for pursuing this resolution.

PETER AND STEPHANIE SILVA

Peter and Stephanie Silva had built remarkable lives.

High-school sweethearts, the couple had married the summer after graduation, and Peter, needing a regular paycheck, began working at his family's office supply store directly after the wedding. Stephanie joined him, and over the next thirty-five years, while raising three children, the couple built the small retail store that Peter's parents had started into a nationwide company.

Peter and Stephanie were partners in every sense of the word: they were devoted to their three children and five grandchildren, they shared the same values, and despite their success they still preferred simple pleasures. As Stephanie told me in our first meeting: "We get invited to these fancy charity events, and people are talking about all these sophisticated things. Meanwhile Peter and I feel like yelling—'Hey, where's the beer and the hot dogs?'"

Three years before I met them, Peter and Stephanie had sold their business, and now they spent their time traveling and getting together with family. They also hoped to get to know each other better, which was what brought them to talk with me. Close friends had told them that I had helped their troubled marriage, and Peter and Stephanie thought the idea of weekly talk a good one. "Kind of like having coffee together with somebody there to listen," Stephanie said. "I guess it's an expensive cup of coffee, but what the heck, we can afford it."

Over our first few months of meeting together the conversation covered the couple's feelings about their children, their deliberations about financial matters, considerations regarding their aging parents, and even sex, which they hoped to become more open about. They also told me about some earlier troubles. One particularly rough stretch had come when they learned that Kyle, their oldest son, was gay, and Peter, much more than Stephanie, had trouble accepting him.

"It didn't just affect their relationship," Stephanie told me, "it affected ours. We grew up in a wealthy, white town, and if there had been any tracks we would have been from the other side of them. Especially Peter, not only because his parents owned a retail store, but because he's Portuguese. I figured of all people he should know how it feels to be different."

"To say she wasn't happy would be an understatement," Peter recalled, wincing at the memory. "I knew she was right, but I just couldn't talk about it. I can deal with practical issues, but emotional stuff, that's always been Stephanie's thing. Thankfully she kept after me."

This episode, though difficult, illustrated much that was good about Peter and Stephanie's relationship. The couple had been unafraid to talk to each other when one or another of their troubles or shortcomings emerged—Peter's shyness, his occasional temper, and his inclination to become a bit hardheaded in his decision-making, or Stephanie's frequent feelings of not being very smart, along with her occasional bouts of depression and anxiety—and so they were able to help each other stay on track. I felt privileged to be included in their discussions, and once I managed to suspend my need to be helpful ("Jesus, Doc, I thought you were supposed to listen to *us* talk"), the conversation flowed openly and smoothly.

Several months after we began talking, however, things took a surprising turn. Peter and Stephanie returned from a trip to

Portugal and Ireland, the birthplaces of their respective grand-parents, and they noticed that something felt amiss:

"When we came back we started asking ourselves, 'So what do we do next?'" Peter said. "Take another fancy trip? Sched-ule more sessions with you? All I really know is that I need to go on a diet; I think I've put on twenty pounds since I retired. You know what I think I feel? I've never been bored before, so I don't really know how to recognize the feeling, but I think I'm bored."

"He's right," Stephanie added. "Back when we were building the company and raising the kids we didn't have a choice about getting up at five in the morning and working until eleven at night. It was hard, but we were really happy. Now we'll never have to worry about money again—neither will our kids for that matter—but it feels like there's something wrong with how we're living."

REAL SELVES, HUMBLE SELVES

Peter and Stephanie were technically baby boomers, but in many ways they had grown up according to the principles of the generation before them—the generation that Tom Brokaw called "The Greatest Generation."[2] They had devoted their lives to work and family, and, like many people of significant accom-plishment, they didn't consider their achievements to have been particularly remarkable. "It didn't seem like a big deal because we never really had a choice," Peter said. "It's something I never understood about some of the young people we hired fresh out of business school. They were smart and knowledgeable, but they didn't have to work as hard as we did, and some of them seemed to take their opportunities for granted."

Now, however, Peter and Stephanie were the ones who didn't have to work. They would never have to worry about money, never, if they chose, be obligated to anyone or anything beyond themselves. As Peter put it in his characteristically gruff way, "The same people who wouldn't give us the time of day because we didn't go to Harvard, now they're kissing our asses because we're rich."

Sounds wonderful, doesn't it? To never again have a financial worry? But in fact Peter and Stephanie had succeeded themselves into a problem; as I've seen time and time again among my wealthier clients, and particularly among their children, great financial success brings with it significant challenges. Why? Once again we come to that central and repeating premise: if our lives are to have real and enduring meaning, we must collide repeatedly with constraint and limitation. Or as Stephanie put it, "We didn't know how good we had it when things were harder."

This matter of how reckoning with reality can help us to grow is so important that it is worth examining through yet one more lens: that of the often used and often misunderstood concept of "selfhood."

The ability to care for and nurture our selves is a surprisingly recent privilege. Notions of "self" did not take root in Europe until between the fifteenth and seventeenth centuries,[3] when advances in standards of living gave people the opportunity to move up the hierarchy of needs from sheer survival to something approaching self-actualization. Times have changed, however, and now such notions as to "be oneself," to "know oneself," and to "express oneself" seem inalienable rights. Indeed, the pendulum has swung so completely that we have become confused about where healthy selfhood ends, and where unhealthy self-centeredness begins.

Selfhood is a deeply complex matter, one that has spawned countless books, songs, poems, theological tracts, and articles in scientific journals, but the essentials of a healthy self can be specified with surprising ease.

When we are talking about a "healthy sense of self":

✧ We're not talking about the self-indulgent, externalizing, entitled selves of our modern "we can have it all and if we don't someone or something is to blame" mind-set, we're talking about selves with enough continuity, solidity, and vitality to be generative, to be generous, to be authentic, to be altruistic, and to genuinely love.

✧ We're not talking about selves that are safely insulated by the illusion of perfectibility, we're talking about selves that grow by virtue of their openness to their own human imperfection.

✧ And we're not talking about selves that trumpet their accomplishments, we're talking about "selves" that have enough substance and solidity to cede center stage, and, ironically enough, to be less obsessed with their own *self*-importance.

Simply put, healthy selfhood has absolutely nothing to do with the "It's all about me" attitude that seems to permeate our society, it is based on a more quiet, more encompassing sense of personal solidity.

So what makes for a healthy sense of self?[4] Well, this too is an obviously complicated question, one determined by a confluence of individual, social, constitutional, and psychological factors, but here again a few simple principles tell us most of what we need to know.

✧ Early on healthy selves are nourished by the love and kindness of parents and other caregivers.

✧ They are supported by biologically based constitutions that have the capacity to tolerate life's expectably painful feelings, thus giving minds the room to grow strong and solid.

⬦ They are helped when they have the good fortune to grow up in environments that respond to their authenticity with validation rather than criticism or shaming.

⬦ And they are further sustained through adulthood by honesty, self-examination, compassion toward one's self and others, self-respect, and self-awareness.

And then there is another factor, one that is perhaps less evident than the preceding, but that is no less important: persons with solid selves also have a deep and abiding ability to see themselves in perspective, largely without grandiosity or self-denigration. In brief, persons with healthy senses of self possess humility.

Humility: often we think of humility as merely a matter of decorum, but in fact humility can be an extraordinary force in our efforts to feel good and to live well. When our senses of self are governed by humility we are able to see beyond our own relatively narrow needs and agendas in order to appreciate the value of persons, principles, and ideas in their own right. We are able, it follows, to love more deeply, to be more passionate, and to live more fully.

We are able to let life truly matter.

And the most direct path to such humility? To believe in something more important than ourselves. Perhaps more than any other of the eight resolutions noted in these pages, this resolution— which aims to capture the deeper meaning of humility—guards against the ubiquitous and life-narrowing trap of self-centeredness. And in doing so it also encourages us to risk exploring the intimate edges that lead to genuine and enduring self-growth.

To illustrate, let's return to Peter and Stephanie's story.

Unretiring

Peter and Stephanie were pretty clear about the problem: "We've got to find something to throw ourselves into again," Stephanie said. "But how do we do that? I'm not really interested in starting another company."

"Aren't there other things worth throwing yourselves into?" I asked.

"What would we do?" Peter answered. "We were good at building a business. We don't know much about anything else."

Peter did believe that he and Stephanie had little to contribute; for all of their success, the couple still held on to strong streaks of insecurity. Peter had been a reliable, well-liked boss, but, his marriage excepted, he was uncomfortable in his relationships. (Probably his biggest obstacle in dealing with Kyle's homosexuality had been his lack of comfort talking about anything personal, much less something as loaded as his own son's sexuality.) Stephanie, meanwhile, trusted her common sense, but she believed that the brainpower behind their company's success belonged to her husband, and she grossly underestimated her own contribution.

For the first time in our relationship, I confronted Peter and Stephanie.

"I don't buy this 'We don't know much about anything else' business," I said playfully. Then, turning more serious, I added: "You've both led remarkable lives. But like all of us you play this kind of shell game where you put your strengths forward, and you hide your insecurities behind them. Maybe it's time to get to know the parts of yourselves that you feel *insecure* about."

"What do you think we feel insecure about?" Stephanie asked.

"Probably different for each of you. Peter is pretty shy when it comes to his more intimate relationships. I know things are better with Kyle, for example, but it's more like a truce than a real resolution." Now, addressing Peter directly, I asked: "I wonder what your life would be like if you pushed yourself to go deeper in your relationships?" Then, turning to Stephanie, I added: "And what would it feel like if you got rid of this image of yourself as just some hardworking, working-class woman whose husband made it big? What if you admitted to yourself that you're pretty darn smart?"

After nearly a minute I broke the silence. "So what do you think?"

"I'd really like my relationships to be closer," Peter answered, his voice sober and even a little sad. "I'd be more like my father. He was never a great success, but he could talk to anybody about anything. And as for Stephanie, we did what we did together. I wish that she knew that."

So Peter and Stephanie set out to write the next chapter in their lives. They considered funding and running their own charitable foundation, but decided that this wouldn't challenge them in the places they'd resolved to change—Peter's shyness, and Stephanie's feelings of intellectual inadequacy. "I don't see where having people come to us asking us for money is going to test us," Peter said. "I figure it would be pretty much a dog-and-pony show."

They considered consulting to other small businesses, but this idea also lacked legs. "It seems like the whole point is finding something new," Stephanie said. "I'm afraid that would just be much more of the same."

As is often the case, Peter and Stephanie's eventual solution came from a personal and painful place: their feelings about their "wrong side of the tracks" backgrounds. They remembered the put-downs, the conversations that stopped as they walked down the school hallways, the condescending surprise some of their teachers showed when they scored well on tests. "You couldn't really put your finger on how they did it," Stephanie remembered, "but they made me feel so dirty that every day the first thing I did when I came home from school was take a shower."

Over the years Peter and Stephanie had used these slights to drive themselves, and now they turned one more time to these old hurts and insecurities for motivation. Forty years after having themselves been underprivileged kids, they decided to make things easier for youngsters in situations similar to their own.

They began by selling the business community on their idea. Through their many contacts they signed up several companies to hire disadvantaged youngsters into a work-study program. The kids would gain valuable experience (the jobs were educational and challenging), contacts, and scholarship money. The businesses would gain positive publicity, and they could defray some of their costs with funds that they received from Peter and Stephanie's program.

Then they enlisted the local school system. Peter and Stephanie had contributed generously to their town and to their old school over the years, and this helped them to cut through the expectable red tape. They got the school to sponsor their program, among other things by giving academic credit for participation.

And then they sold the idea to the kids.

As I mentioned, Peter had always been rather shy. Now he pushed himself to get deeply involved with the teenagers who entered the program. He urged them to go to college, noting that, for all his success, he had always felt inadequate for not having gone himself. The program that he and Stephanie had built, he argued, would make an often unfair process slightly more fair. Participation would help kids develop contacts and references; would provide them with access to private college counselors, standardized test tutors, and other of the advantages that their wealthier peers had; and would help defray the costs of college: a significant aspect of Peter and Stephanie's proposal was the accrual of scholarship funds, some of which were earned through working, and much of which came from money donated to the program.

Meanwhile, as Peter got to know "his kids," learning about their backgrounds and their struggles, becoming involved with their families, and being the person many turned to when things got tough, Stephanie dealt with businesses, with educational boards, and with government regulations regarding nonprofit organizations. In her own words, she did the "smart-person" work that Peter had previously done.

Within two years Peter and Stephanie had built an organization in which disadvantaged kids could feel pride and ownership. Theirs was a program that did the world a great deal of good, while also giving them the opportunity to remain active and vital well into their supposed "retirement."

Peter described it well when, several months after we had stopped our regular meetings, he and Stephanie returned "just to check in": "You know, maybe I'm just not that thoughtful a person," he said, "but I'm not sure I agree with that saying: 'The unexamined life is not worth living.' I think I'm happiest when I'm solving a problem. And the best times Stephanie and I have had have come when we're solving problems together."

FROM HUMILITY TO GENERATIVITY

Erik Erikson considered one of the central tasks of growing older to be that of achieving "generativity";[5] embracing one's fallibility and one's humanity, appreciating with realism one's place in the larger order, and using one's accrued wisdom to make the world a better place for others.

The first vestige of "generativity" often occurs around the births of our children when we feel, in many instances for the first time, that there are lives that matter more than our own. Over time the deep and relatively selfless feelings that we have for our children (feelings that seemed to be missing for Clara and Austin) expand to our grandchildren, and they even, if our maturity and wisdom continue to grow, extend beyond our own families to our fellow man.

Sound naively altruistic? In many ways such selflessness also works for us. Caring about persons and principles other than ourselves helps us with two of midlife's most difficult challenges: to prepare for our own deaths, and to appreciate our lives in ways that are quite different from the way that we did when we were younger.

Let's begin with the seemingly daunting proposition of facing the fact that we have limited time left.

Selflessness and humility play critical roles in our efforts not only to accept, but even to embrace, the finite nature of our lives. Recognizing that we are not the centers of the universe that our younger selves often felt themselves to be makes it easier to let go of the life we have held so tightly. And understanding that there are persons and principles that are more important than ourselves makes it possible to graciously and generously cede center stage to the next generation.

And then there is the way that seeing ourselves in scale also helps us to find different, and in many ways more grounded, joys and satisfactions as we grow older.

During our twenties, thirties, and forties our omnipotent strivings can fuel our ambitions, often leading us to real accomplishments. If we don't eventually learn to see ourselves in scale, however, we will forever measure ourselves against an impossible standard, and, it follows, feel that we have come up short.

Humility allows us to judge ourselves more kindly. When we are able to see ourselves accurately in relation to the world around us, we can appreciate ourselves, and our accomplishments, more realistically. And so we can value such simple and private human achievements as raising families, doing meaningful work that never achieves public recognition, having good relationships, and touching individual lives. We can, as did Peter and Stephanie, find happiness by immersing ourselves in causes about which we are passionate.

We can become our most genuine, and least narcissistic, selves.

BELIEVING *TOGETHER* IN SOMETHING MORE IMPORTANT THAN OURSELVES

We tend to know our spouses better than we know anyone else. We tend to be better known by our spouses than we are by anyone else. We know each other's strengths and each other's fault lines, and we know what matters most to each other. Such intimate knowledge often makes our relationships very difficult, but here again potential trouble can be turned into powerful opportunity: because we know each other's vulnerabilities and strengths inside out, we are uniquely equipped to support and challenge each other. We can help each other to achieve the kind of growth that comes when we are willing to open ourselves in those places that we are most driven to avoid.

The resolutions outlined in this book should not necessarily be considered achievable absolutes, rather they are best thought of as North Stars that we know to look for when we have lost our way. As intimate partners we can use our unique influence to help each other to search for, and to find, these North Stars. They are designed to lead us out of complacency, and into those places in ourselves that we need to embrace if we are to keep growing, and keep changing.

So how do we help each other to be more humble, and to believe in something more important than ourselves?

- **Work together to create a lifestyle that supports altruism, service, and generativity.** The rewards that come from pursuing these values are not the quick fixes that we so often crave. But they are deeper and more enduring.
- **Help each other maintain perspective on the more superficial measures of success.** In this society it is hard not to feel lousy about yourself when you don't keep up with the Joneses, but if your spouse really doesn't need you to drive a fancy car, then you'll have an easier time not driving that car. Better yet, if your spouse loves you all the more for driving that old beater, well, it makes it a lot easier to drive that old beater.
- **Don't be afraid to call each other on your conceits and grandiosities.** We all have them, to greater and lesser degrees. We tend to avoid confronting them in each other, fearing that we will in turn be called on ours. Go ahead, find playful and compassionate ways to call each other on your narcissism. Keep each other grounded. Ask each other to maintain a sense of humility.
- **Make conversations about values, politics, and larger social issues part of your relationship.** The older we get, the more inclined we are to retreat into our own comfort zones. The better off we are, the more we have the resources to allow these retreats. Encourage each other to go in the opposite direction: don't be isolated, be involved.
- As you get older, and as some of the demands of raising children recede, **fill the space with something other than self-interest.**

    ✦ Revive your principles.

    ✦ Do community service *together*.

    ✦ Give to charity.

- **Become the person that your partner will want to share his or her dreams with.**
- **Don't put too much emphasis on seeking happiness directly.** Happiness is a by-product of a well-lived life, not a goal, and it is achieved through the pursuit of endeavors that are meaningful and even, ironically, sometimes painful.

And if you're going alone:

- Once again, **first look inward.** Confront your own self-centeredness.
- Rather than asking your partner to be his or her best self, **ask your partner to help you be your best self.** Say: "I want to start living differently. I'd like to pursue some things that matter to me, and that I haven't made myself pursue. You don't have to join me if you don't want to, but I'd like it if you did."
- If your partner won't join you, go ahead and **be the better person** anyway. Don't gloat or judge, just model. Model, model, and then model some more. Your partner will eventually have to make a choice—join you, or lose you.

A Reassuring Sense of Smallness

"My husband died last week."

His neighbor had waved to him, as she had so many mornings over the past twenty years, at the intersection of his morning run and her morning walk to pick up the newspaper on her front lawn. Unlike their usual passing greetings, however, this time she had waved him over. That was when she told him.

"I'm so sorry. Are you OK?"

"I'm OK. You know I haven't really had him for five years."

He understood. Twenty years ago when they had first moved to the neighborhood, her husband—"The Doctor," he and his wife had respectfully called him—had been the one to run by *their* house each morning. As the years passed, and as their kids had been born and then grown older, his runs had slowed into walks, but he still kept that lively stride and that bright and immediate face. Then five years ago he went missing for a few months. When he reappeared it was in a wheelchair, his wife pushing him down the same route he'd run so often. For the first few years he still offered that bright "hello," but as the years went by and as the ambulances had stopped at his house with increasing regularity, he seemed to be less and less aware. Yet even then, even though his brain had clearly stopped working, his face still gave off that same bright immediacy.

"Will you let us know if there's anything we can do?"

"I'm OK. I've been mostly managing by myself for some time, you know."

He was relieved by her answer. All through his run he'd been mired in that grinding irritation he felt when he was tired from work, when he resented the hours, and when the money never quite seemed to be enough. In truth he probably wouldn't have asked if he hadn't already known that she would say "no."

A few minutes later he walked into his house. His wife was sitting at the kitchen table, paying bills.

"The Doctor died," he told her. He didn't feel like talking; when he felt this way it seemed too much of an effort to make the effort, but he knew that not telling her would do an injustice to their relationship. They had quietly shared their admiration of the man for the past twenty years; two adults who never quite felt like adults, they found his proximity reassuring.

She didn't look up from the checks she was writing, but he could tell that she'd heard him because she became very still. After a few moments she looked up and found his eyes: "He seemed like such a nice man," she said sadly. "I always imagined he lived a good life."

Her words cleared the resentment from his brain. He pictured *her* wheeling *him* down the street, blanket over his lap to shield him from the fall chill (maybe it would be the other way around, but somehow he had always imagined he would be the one to go first). He saw himself scowling at the neighborhood kids for being too noisy—a far cry from the Doctor's bright hello. He laughed at himself—most of the time he took himself far too seriously, he thought—and with this his irritation gave way to sadness.

"Do you remember when we first bought the house?" he asked. "How that first night we slept here we wondered whether this was where we would die?"

She nodded, waiting for him to continue, but he was lost in his own thoughts again. This morning, in this house, with this woman who was his wife, with two kids off in college, one in New York and one on the West Coast, he could feel the life that they had built together. He imagined his kids coming back for his funeral, surely being sad, but then returning to their lives. It was odd that thoughts of his death would disburden him of his tension and irritation, but they did. They brought him a reassuring sense of smallness. The pettiness, the worrying, the oppressive self-importance—he could let them all go in the momentary knowledge of his own impermanence.

CHAPTER VI

GIVE UP YOUR HABITS
AND ADDICTIONS

If you give a mouse a food pellet every time it pushes a bar, it will learn to push that bar on its own. If you give that mouse a pellet every fifth time it pushes the bar, it will push the bar more frequently. And if you want to get that mouse to spend the rest of its life doing little else but pushing that bar, reward its bar-pushes occasionally and somewhat unpredictably: it will be hooked for life. Behavioral psychologists call this last paradigm a variable reinforcement schedule, and it's the most powerful way we know to ingrain a behavior. It's the reason that gambling is so addictive, and it's also the reason that we Red Sox fans kept coming back for more all those years.[1]

It's hardly news that reward systems play a critical role in our habits and our choices; most of us understand that we tend to do what feels good again, and we tend not to do what feels bad. What *is* news to most of us, however, is the degree to which *normal* reward-seeking behaviors can have insidiously adverse consequences. And these consequences only get worse as we grow older.

Here's how:

First of all, reward and reinforcement paradigms tend to be extremely shortsighted. Just as a mouse will prefer a bar that delivers a single pellet immediately over one that yields five pellets an hour later, we humans tend to choose more easily attainable and more immediately gratifying rewards over more difficult to obtain but potentially more enduring satisfactions. From opting for that extra burger (even though we know we need to lose a few pounds) to buying that sports car (even though we're behind in saving for retirement), the laws of learned behavior time and time again cause us to make the kind of quick-fix choices that run counter to what is best for our long-term well-being.

And then there's the part where things only get worse as we get older. Over time we accumulate behaviors that make us feel good (and, importantly, that help us to avoid feeling bad). By midlife, it follows, we have accumulated a very large catalogue of such behaviors.

So what's so bad about feeling good? Nothing, in and of itself—feeling good is generally good, and not feeling bad is generally good.

But feeling good is only part of life's equation.

Living well as we get older involves tolerating discomfort and risk in order to keep growing.[2] Unfortunately, our tendency to seek short-term rewards, coupled with our inclination to steer away from growth-promoting discomfort, leads us to predictability, complacency, and repetition—qualities that are hardly conducive to such growth. Our aging well-being, therefore, requires that we make a purposeful commitment to trade in some of our precious short-term pleasures for deeper, less immediate satisfactions.

Give up your habits and addictions. This is the sixth resolution. To be sure, it's not easy to stretch ourselves beyond our familiar comfort zones (as Bette Davis noted, "Getting old is not for sissies"). Our long-term relationships, however, can help us to make the harder choices that can, in turn, make growing older a time of expanding, rather than diminishing, possibility.

CHET AND LINDA BRANSON

On first meeting, Chet and Linda Branson seemed a remarkably unremarkable couple. Chet was a trim, neatly dressed man whose blond hair showed a touch of gray. Linda was a diminutive woman who arrived at my office in sneakers, jeans, and a loose sweater, and she tied her long brown hair, also streaked with gray, back in a bun. Linda seemed to have a bit more spark than Chet, at least in a relative sort of way. While Chet was deferentially polite, Linda joked about my office, noting that my analytic couch made her wonder whether she had walked into a *New Yorker* cartoon.

"It's not like anything is terribly wrong," Linda began. "We don't fight, we mostly agree about how to raise our daughter, and we care about each other. But we don't talk, and we don't have much fun together. In fact life in general doesn't feel like a whole lot of fun these days. I'm not even sure that couples therapy is what we need, but if we could make our relationship better it would at least be a step."

Chet and Linda had met eight years previously, when both were in their early forties. After dating for about a year they had married, and two years after that, after a year of trying, and failing, to conceive a biological child, they adopted a one-year-old girl from Eastern Europe. When they came to see me their daughter, Natasha, had just turned three.

Had they been happy early on in their relationship, I wondered?

"'Happy' is not a word I often use to describe myself," Chet answered. "I think that Linda would say the same."

I had only just met Chet and Linda, but I could sense what he meant. Some people expect more from life than it can reasonably offer, and these folks struggle with the disparity between their expectations and their realities. Others expect less than what is possible, and they live relatively small and unfulfilling lives because they don't ask life for enough. Chet, who made a modest but dependable living working for an advertising agency, and Linda, who did likewise as an accountant, seemed to fit squarely into the latter category.

Neither Chet nor Linda had been in therapy before, and both seemed interested in using the first several sessions to talk about their individual backgrounds. I learned that Chet's father had abandoned the family when Chet was eight. Father and son didn't speak to each other again until Chet was twenty-eight, when the older man, homeless and severely alcoholic, called to ask him for money. Chet's father may have been physically absent, but his specter dominated the household. "Not a day went by when my mother didn't bring him up," Chet said. "'Be responsible. Don't be like your father.' That was all I ever heard. The idea that life could be fun was simply not part of the deal."

As I listened I began to understand how Chet had learned to live so small. He was terrified of failing to fulfill his responsibilities, like his father, and so he took on as little as he possibly could—at his job, with Linda, and even with Natasha, whose parenting he left largely to his wife. His basic guiding principle, it appeared, was "If I don't try I can't fail."

If Chet was afraid of responsibility, then Linda was afraid of being in a relationship. "I figured I'd wait until I was about forty-five and then I'd adopt," she admitted. "If anybody came along that I liked, fine, but I wasn't really looking for it."

Linda came by her fears honestly. Her father had been a domineering man who complained bitterly whenever he didn't get his way. Linda's mother had been overwhelmed by her husband's tyranny and by the demands of her four children, and Linda, the oldest, had held the family together. Her toughest job was that of surviving her father's overbearing need to have everything revolve around him.

"When I'm intimate with a man I feel like I'm a bunch of iron filings and the guy is the magnet," she said. "When Chet's not around I'm fine, and when I don't share anything with him I'm OK, but if I start to need him or depend on him, it feels like everything that's me gets pulled toward him, and I lose my center."

Both Chet and Linda had chosen partners that they assumed to be safe (safety, you will see, proved to be both Chet and Linda's preferred "pellet"). Chet entered the relationship fearful of taking on any responsibility, and he had chosen a wife who was unlikely to ask very much of him. Linda, who feared losing herself to a man's demands, had chosen a husband on whom she was unlikely to rely.

Unfortunately, as is usually the case when we choose our partners out of fear rather than desire, neither Chet nor Linda were getting what they really *needed* from each other, and both felt lonely, disappointed, and increasingly unhappy.

A Confederacy of Distance

After several weeks of telling their individual stories, Chet and Linda began to shift their focus toward their relationship. Not surprisingly, Linda made the first foray into trying to change things. The subject was Chet's relationship with pornography. Linda began by noting that while she had moral reservations about pornography, she also felt that people had the right to do as they chose in the privacy of their own homes. What was more, the "stuff" that Chet looked at was largely "white-bread," and he wasn't particularly secretive; when he would disappear into the basement to "surf the Net" there was an unspoken understanding between them that much of that surfing involved looking at adult sites. It was one of their many "quasi-secrets," she said.

Why raise the issue now, I wondered.

"Because Natasha is getting older. Maybe a better question, though, would be why I haven't brought it up before. And the answer, I'm realizing, is that I'm not sure I really want to change things. If I'm really honest with myself I have to ask whether I really want him to want sex with me instead of the computer. If he changes, am I willing to change? I have my stuff, too."

"Like your drinking?" Chuck felt defensive and embarrassed, and his voice had more of an edge than did his wife's.

"Does Linda's drinking bother you?" I asked.

"Not really," Chuck answered, his voice softening. "I have my porn in the evenings; she has her booze."

The couple told me about Linda's drinking. She wasn't an alcoholic in the classic sense; she never missed work, never had driven drunk, hadn't had any health problems, and rarely became obviously intoxicated. Nevertheless her nightly two to three glasses of wine were clearly a drug. "I organize my life around it," she acknowledged. "I pour those glasses of wine at night and then I don't have to think about things I should be thinking about."

"So is that how we do it?" she continued, after a momentary pause. "He hides behind his porn, I hide behind my wine?"

It *was* how they did it. Chet ran from the responsibility of being a husband and a father by retreating into his pornography. Linda eased worries that she might otherwise have shared with Chet by fleeing into the sanctuary of her wine. Together, their habits and addictions brought them the kind of quick-fix, life-limiting rewards that habits and addictions invariably tend to bring; in this case, the relief of never having to deal with the painful and complicated feelings that each needed to take on if they were to change and grow.

WHEN WE TRADE SAFETY FOR RISK

We all need safety. We are all, to greater and lesser degrees, motivated by the need for security and protection when we initially choose our partners, and this need plays a similarly central role in shaping subsequent patterns of interaction in our relationships. That we are built this way isn't necessarily bad. Safety is a primary need; security, comfort, and trust are important in and of themselves, and safety also provides a foundation for virtually all that is positive in relationships. Some degree of safety, for example, is a necessary condition if we are to risk expanding our lives beyond our familiar comfort zones, and so to remain vital, to change, and to grow.

At times, however, safety becomes such an overriding concern that the effort to achieve it precludes the possibility of creative risk-taking. Under these circumstances our relationships, and our lives, narrow and deaden.

The laws of behaviorism play a central role in this spiral into stagnation. Once again, we tend to seek short-term rewards over longer-term, more complex satisfactions. Over time we develop ever-expanding catalogues of behaviors that will elicit such rewards, and that will also steer us away from pain and discomfort. We become increasingly reliant on our habits and addictions, and we retreat ever further into the feel-good safety of our familiar comfort zones.

Given that the key to aging well may quite possibly be reduced to a few simple words—keep growing and keep changing—this is very bad news for us middle-aged baby boomers.

Fortunately, where there is bad news there is also good news. If we choose (and I will argue that *choose* is indeed the right word) to make a shared commitment to being real and vulnerable with each other in minds, selves, and bodies, if we jointly agree *not* to retreat into our familiar safety zones, we can, together, reverse our natural tendency to get smaller as we get older.

Giving Up Old Habits and Addictions, Renegotiating Old Agreements

For a full year I talked to Chet about his fear of responsibility. I continuously reminded him that while retreat from being a father and a husband eased this fear in the short run, in the long run it caused him to be more, rather than less, like his father. I urged him to reach out to Linda and Natasha, and to risk *not* being "good enough" for them. I challenged Linda similarly. Sure, Chet had his problems, but being a demanding tyrant like her father was not one of them. I urged her to risk asking her husband for what she needed; he might not come through, but she didn't have to lose her autonomy and selfhood to him.

Most importantly, I repeatedly suggested to both that the first step in changing things would be to give up their nightly addictions to pornography and wine.

Over time, Linda became cognizant of how she didn't ask Chet for help with Natasha, or ask him to hold her or talk to her when she was unhappy. She also became mindful of the cause of her reluctance; her fear, dating back to her relationship with her father, that she would "owe" for whatever she received. "Whenever my father did anything for me, if he bought me something, even if it was something really basic like books for school, he expected something in return," she said. "And what he expected most of all was for me to be exactly the way *he* thought I should be."

Chet, in turn, acknowledged how much his fear of failing in his responsibilities caused him to withdraw from Linda and Natasha. "I'll be in the basement on the computer, half doing some designs for work and half just surfing all those sites you guys know about, and I'll hear Linda putting Natasha to bed. I know I should get my ass out of that chair and help, but it's like I physically can't move. I know it's nuts, but I still feel like if I don't get involved in the first place I can't let them down."

Chet and Linda were increasingly clear about what they were doing, and why they were doing it. The therapy, it appeared, was working. But for one problem: they weren't changing.

"At this point we basically understand the problem," Linda noted. "It works better for him if I'm a hard-assed bitch who does everything herself because responsibility freaks him out. It works better for me to have him be some useless perv jerking off in the basement because *I* freak out at the thought of depending on him." Linda paused for a moment, a sad smile softening her harsh words. "So we get it. That's who we were when we got married, and we've only made each other more that way over time. So how do we change it?"

Help from a Child

Sometimes when we are most stuck, help comes from an unexpected source. For Chet and Linda that help came from Natasha, their daughter.

"We have something to show you," Linda said, some eighteen months into the therapy. She opened the old, frayed backpack that she carried (the pack was a vestige of the year she had spent traveling after college; the one time in her life, she told us, that she truly felt free), and she took out a manila folder.

"Natasha started kindergarten last week. Here's her first homework." Linda opened the folder, and handed me a child's drawing. "The assignment was to draw your family."

I looked at the drawing. There were three small human figures, artistically drawn for a five-year-old. A little girl with long brown hair stood in one corner of the page. In another corner, as far from the girl as possible, another lone figure sat in front of a box. The short blond hair indicated that this was a man. In yet another corner, again as distant as possible from the other two figures, a third figure, a woman by virtue of her long brown hair, stood with a glass in her hand.

"So that's what Natasha sees every night," Chet said, after giving me a few moments to study the drawing. "Daddy at his computer, Mommy with her wine, everybody alone."

"It's funny how you can know things and yet not know them,"

he continued. "You can understand that you're living your life all wrong, that you're making all the same mistakes your father made, and yet you can somehow put all that in some closet so it never really hits you. But when I looked at that picture it hit me. Boy did it hit me."

I told Chet that I thought we all had the capacity to know and yet not know things, particularly when *really* knowing meant that we would have to make changes that we were scared to make.

Now it was Linda's turn. "So it's time to do things differently. And we've already started. More because of Chet than because of me. When I saw that picture I cried. Chet didn't say anything, but instead of going down to the basement like he usually does, he helped me put Natasha to bed. Later we sat down and talked. He said we were going to change things, starting with what you've been telling us to do for a year and a half; he was going to give up the evening computer sessions, and I was going to give up the wine. I can have it if we go out to dinner, but the nightly habit stops."

Chet and Linda helped each other to stick with this commitment. Sometimes when things slipped they policed each other, sometimes they supported each other; always they spoke firmly but kindly to each other. Surprisingly, the hardest part wasn't giving up the addictions—Chet found he could live without the pornography, and Linda missed her wine less than she expected—the hardest part was that once they gave up their addictions, their relationship seemed, at least on the surface, to become more difficult.

"I feel like she's pissed off at me all the time," Chet noted, some four months after striking their agreement. "How does that figure, I'm doing better and she's more angry?"

"It actually makes a kind of weird sense," Linda answered. "Before, I never expected anything, and when I started to feel irritated about having to do everything I just poured another glass. Now he's doing a lot more, but I still need more than I'm getting. And on top of that I also want more."

Chet grew silent for a moment, and when he spoke his voice was soft and thoughtful: "The hard part really isn't that she's mad," he said, "it's what's happening inside me. When she's mad I feel like I'm not good enough. I know that some of this is actually just normal stuff that men and women deal with when they have a young kid, but that doesn't help me fight the feeling that I'm just a no-good derelict."

"Like your father," I noted.

"Yeah, like my father."

Husbands and wives are bound together by contracts based on unspoken wishes, fears, and assumptions. Often the most influential and binding of these contracts are those that ensure mutual safety through implicit agreements to stay away from those parts of each other that are most vulnerable and most pained. If relationships are to survive and even thrive, and if individual partners are to find their way to the kinds of intimate interactions that allow new experience and new learning, these initial marital agreements need to be rewritten.

Chet and Linda did just this.

Catalyzed by their daughter's drawing, and organized by a growing understanding of the costs of their arrangements, Chet continued to force himself to become a more available husband and father, and Linda continued to risk relying more on Chet, both for herself and for help with their daughter. These shifts reverberated throughout their relationship, causing further change. As Chet made himself more available, Linda had to come to terms with her fears of depending on him, and as she did she was able to ask Chet for even more. As Linda asked more of Chet, he, in turn, had to grapple with his fear of failing in his responsibilities.

By giving up their habits and addictions, and by replacing these behaviors with newer and more constructive ones, Chet and Linda turned their cycle of self-perpetuating retreat into a cycle of self-perpetuating change.

Six months after Natasha brought her family portrait home, now some two years after we had begun working together, Chet and Linda spoke about the changes that had occurred.

"In some ways I don't feel all that different," Linda began, "but when I take a step back I can see how much things have changed from the way they were three years ago. Take what happened last Tuesday. I had to stay late at work. In the past I would have gone home and then gone back to work later, I would have found any way I could to not need Chet, even if it meant bending myself into a pretzel. But instead I called him at work to see if he could get home early. I could tell he was a little peeved, but he said OK."

"Sorry about that," Chet said. "I've been more serious at work lately, and I was pretty tired. But it really was OK. Like we've been saying in here, what's been happening is hard sometimes, but it's good."

We both knew what Chet meant. He had been telling us recently about how anxious he felt, about how he frequently doubted himself, about how he no longer felt comfortably numb. And yet, he had told us, there were also moments when he could feel enormously gratified that he was choosing a path quite different from his father.

"Actually, your reaction was OK. In fact that's sort of my point. I could tell that you weren't happy at first, and I had this moment of feeling 'I'll owe him,' 'Forget it'—all the old stuff. But I talked myself through it, Chet stayed with it, and it all worked out.

"And here's the really neat thing," Linda continued. "Not only did I get some help, I felt like I could trust him. And that was *really* nice."

CHOOSING OUR BEST SELVES

We baby boomers have been exposed to various theories about how we change. First there was psychoanalysis, pretty much the only game in town when we were younger. Psychoanalysis, and the various forms of therapy that evolved from it, taught us that change occurs by engaging in a long relationship with a therapist who will help us to understand the historical roots of our maladaptive patterns.[3]

Then self-help became a prominent influence on our assumptions regarding change. Alas self-help, which began as a thoughtful alternative to psychoanalysis, evolved into a largely superficial approach that, like the old joke about Chinese food, left us hungry an hour later.

More recently psychiatric medications became the holy grail of personal change. There is no doubt that drugs can offer some degree of relief to those suffering from major psychiatric disorders, but the promise of pills as a panacea for everyday human suffering has proven to be a false one.

And most recently mystical and spiritual influences have taken center stage. Many of these use age-old Eastern notions of mindfulness and meditation. Others try to sell us the ultimate quick-fix notion that our wishes and intentions can be magically transformed into results.

If we are confused about how we change and grow, we have good reason: there are thousands of vendors of personal growth out there, each claiming that his product is the best. Even worse, all of the aforementioned approaches can, at their worst, promote the very attitudes that good help should enable us to overcome: they seduce us into imagining that growth is possible without making painful choices, and they perpetuate the illusion that our selves are perfectible. (We all could've been contenders[4] if only we had found enough kindness and understanding, been given the proper advice, or been prescribed the right drug.)

Clearly there are countless ways that we change, many of them quite useful. No single way is best for everyone, and what's more, what may be best at one moment in our lives may not be best at another. A few simple principles, however, govern all useful approaches to personal change and improvement:

◇ All meaningful solutions are deeply personal and hard-earned (there are no "one-size-fits-all" answers).

◇ Personal growth requires commitment over time.

◇ All meaningful change requires confronting parts of one's own self that will resist the very changes one intends to make.

◇ All change comes with a price (you have to give something up in order to get something new).

◇ The changes we make in our personalities tend to be small: we are, by and large, who we are.

◇ At the same time, even the smallest changes in our selves can lead to life-altering differences in our lives.

Then add to this list one more critical point: change involves choosing, by dint of our own free wills, the paths we wish to take.

This seemingly obvious principle is surprisingly absent from many of the more established models of change, an oversight that explains why therapy and self-help so often create states of over-dependence and self-indulgence; if change occurs less through our own wills and resources than through the ministrations of a magically endowed helper, then it naturally follows that we will cede, rather than take, responsibility for our lives.

Choice, not the limitless possibility to choose whatever one wants, but choice that involves both realistic possibilities and also inevitable, and sometimes painful, costs and consequences, is a powerful antidote to self-indulgence and entitlement. This kind of choice—which requires us to know our patterns, see their costs, and then actively embark on a path that will help us to make necessary changes—is an underappreciated aspect of change and growth.

THE MARRIAGE BENEFIT: CHOOSING CHANGE TOGETHER

Sounds simple, doesn't it? Know your patterns, see their costs, and then make the necessary changes. If change is this straightforward, why don't we all do it, and why don't we do it without all that expensive help?

Here's why not.

Chet and Linda didn't come up with their maladaptive patterns because they were stupid or stubborn; their self-limiting ways of relating were, in fact, the best solutions they could find for the dilemmas they faced earlier in their lives. That they had been able to marry and have a child was already an accomplishment. Becoming more intimate, more dependable, and more reliant would have meant giving up their favored solutions and facing their greatest fears. That, at the time they came to see me, was more than they could manage.

We all have to negotiate this same basic dilemma: meaningful change is hard because the patterns and behaviors that we most need to change are also, invariably, our most dependable ways of not experiencing our greatest fears, our most painful feelings, and our most tender injuries. Change and growth, it follows, demand that we let go of our most reliable solutions (which often means giving up our habits and addictions), and that we tolerate the very fears, feelings, and injuries that we most want to avoid.

OK, but what does all this have to do with our long-term intimate relationships?

There is a story, perhaps apocryphal, about a harrowing dilemma faced by the *Apollo 13* astronauts:[5] if they entered the atmosphere too steeply they would encounter more friction than their space capsule could withstand, and they would burn up. If they entered at too shallow an angle they would skip off the atmosphere like a flat stone on still water, and, not having enough fuel to try another reentry, would be forever entombed in space. To a man they preferred the former death to the latter—there was something about the aloneness of eternal space that was intolerable. I suspect that this is the same reason that the vast majority of suicides on the Golden Gate Bridge take place looking toward the city rather than the ocean; we humans desperately want to feel connected.

We feel this need for contact and connection even more strongly when we set out to do hard things. Therefore, if we are going to take the risk of letting go of our self-limiting but self-protective patterns, and if we are going to risk facing those aspects of our experience that we are most loath to face, we will need the help of our fellow humans.

What better help could there be than that of our life partner?

Of course there is a significant fly in this ointment. It's all well and good to say that we can lean on the love and trust of our intimate partners as we embark on the hard work of changing ourselves, but as we all know, relationships are often difficult. What's more, as Chet and Linda's story illustrates, we often enlist our partners in a mutual agreement NOT to change.

Well, here's where once again the bad news can also be good news. Intimate relationships are built, among other things, upon foundations of shared or complementary injuries. Over time we weave ourselves together in a fabric of patterns and habits that are designed to hide those injuries. Every change we make, it follows, reverberates through our relationships, rewriting old contracts, changing old habits, and destabilizing old patterns, thus causing long-closeted vulnerabilities to emerge.

In other words, it is precisely *because* we get stuck together that we are also uniquely equipped to unstick each other.

So what are some pragmatic steps we can take to give up our habits and addictions, and so to open ourselves to change and growth?

- We are all afraid of something. We all contort our lives, and ourselves, in our efforts to avoid these fears. **Know your fears,** and make a point of moving toward them rather than away from them.
- **Identify the behaviors that you use to avoid these fears.** These behaviors can range from subtle habits to overt addictions. Be as honest as you can possibly be about the ways that you narrow and limit your life in order to avoid changing what you need to change.
- **Take stock together.** Agree to talk to each other about your self-limiting and self-protective patterns. When you do this emphasize your own patterns, rather than your partner's.
- **Assume that you will underestimate your reliance on drugs, alcohol, and other forms of addiction.** Alcohol, for example, is a costly solution long before the formal criteria for alcoholism are met. A habitual, nightly glass of wine can be a way of avoiding the very things you most need to deal with.
- **Appreciate how hard it can be to make these changes, and be vocal in appreciating your partner's efforts.**
- **Make deals.** "I'll give up X if you give up Y" can be a very helpful approach.
- **Become each other's habits.** By supporting each other and

encouraging each other, by being there for each other, we can help each other to risk giving up our familiar crutches.

- **Persevere.** Meaningful change takes time. "I quit drinking for Lent and it didn't make any difference" is not good enough. You have to give up the habit, and then you have to live without it for an extended period of time if you are going to change.

And if your partner won't join you?

- If your partner won't give up his or her habits and addictions, **go it alone.** Give up yours, and then stay the course. Once again, model.
- **Don't judge.** Emphasize the positive over the negative. "How about if we do something instead of watching television? Maybe we can talk, maybe go to a movie" is better than, "Why do you sit in front of that television like a slug every night?"
- **Be willing to put the relationship on the table.** If your partner won't change, would you, at some point, be willing to ask yourself whether your relationship is healthy for you? Asking this question does not necessarily mean that you are not committed. It can be a powerful means of breaking old patterns.

Marriage is not therapy, nor should it be. Married partners are probably more likely to become mired in stagnant patterns than are partners in therapy (though mutual stagnation is by no means foreign to therapy). But marriages are also *less* prone than therapy to the kind of imbalance in care and attention that leads to overdependence and self-absorption. And because marriages involve real and intimate contact with a person who is different and separate from us, they can, at their best, offer us the most direct and powerful path to undoing the patterns and habits that narrow our lives.

A Saturday Morning Refuge

Saturday morning. It seemed like things should be different now that Brad was off at college and Jenny had her license. The endless driving of kids that seemed to occupy their weekends was all but gone, and Kendra had imagined that they'd have more time together. But somehow it hadn't worked out that way. Evan was where he usually was on Saturday mornings, upstairs in that windowless little closet he called his "office," maybe paying bills, maybe making calls—she was never quite sure what he did up there.

Evan was, in fact, paying bills, but he was hardly a model of efficiency. The problem with having the finances on the computer was that the Internet was just a click away. Those endless joke lists he'd found his way onto, the news, the sports, even, God help him, the weather; paying the bills tended to devolve into hours of mindless mouse-clicking.

Kendra knew that if she walked upstairs, knocked on the door, playfully called Evan a "mole," and asked him to go for a walk he'd agree. But she was grinding on that old "Why do I have to do all the work in the relationship" feeling, and so while he busied himself with his bills—or so he said—she turned to *her* Saturday morning ritual: reviewing her patients' charts. She didn't really need to—mostly she was just reassuring herself about her own thoroughness—but feeling good about herself as a doctor sure beat the hell out of waiting for Evan.

Evan looked up from the computer while he waited for the new download to finish. His eyes drifted to that familiar photo on his desk. Summer vacation, about fifteen years ago, he guessed. Brad looked like he was about six, which would have made Jenny about three. Christ, he and Kendra looked different back then. "Wonderful times," he thought, but he knew that was just a partial truth. The father in the photo was smiling, but he also had that faraway look in his eyes. All his life—even, and in some ways especially, in the moments that he had been happiest—Evan had been a little bit someplace else. It occurred to him that he was happier in his memories than he had been in the events that those memories recalled.

Evan's mind drifted to earlier that morning, when Kendra had headed for the shower without rolling over to him. He had thought of asking her to wait, to lie with him, maybe they'd have made love, maybe not, but at least they would have seen what might happen. But he had been irritated that she hadn't thought of it herself, so he hadn't said anything. Besides, the idea of slipping into the solitude of his office had been appealing. Now, though, as he looked at the photo, as he focused in on his wife's face, he wanted to talk to her.

Kendra, meanwhile, had quieted her irritation. It didn't take nearly the effort it used to; years ago she could stew for days, but now—she wasn't sure whether it was because she was older and wiser or whether it was because she was older and just more tired of fighting—she found it easier to let it go. And so she headed upstairs to call her husband a "mole."

They met midway, at the landing. Amongst the photographs that lined the stairwell. One winter she had organized all the summer photos in neat, ascending order, so that a walk up the stairs was a walk through the summers of their lives. The pictures stopped when Brad was sixteen, the year that they had stopped bringing the camera.

"Feel like a walk?" The words came out together, and they laughed.

"Do you have time?" Again they spoke together, and again they laughed. They both knew this dance of desire and constraint so well.

"Sure," Evan said. "It's not like the bills won't be there when we get back."

CHAPTER VII

FORGIVE AND GIVE THANKS

Much has been written lately about the importance of forgiveness. Research in behavioral medicine[1] suggests that "overcontrolled hostility" is a significant predictor of heart disease (along the magnitude of smoking and obesity), while lessened hostility is associated with such positive medical indicators as lowered blood pressure and a stronger immune system. The recent resurgence of religion and spirituality has brought with it an increased appreciation of traditional values such as acceptance and forgiveness. And a backlash against our culture of victimization[2] has swung the pendulum away from grievance and revenge. As Ned Hallowell notes in his book *Dare to Forgive*, to let go of anger and resentment through acts of forgiveness is to give up "your title to a polluted pond."

To some, however, all this talk of forgiveness can sound a bit naïve. Doris, a woman with whom I worked for many years, had been raped repeatedly by her father when she was a little girl. "No matter how much work I do on myself, I'll never make love with my husband without seeing a picture of my father," she said. "I'll never look at my daughter without remembering what he did to me. Forgive? I understand that my father was just doing to me what someone did to him, and sometimes I can even feel compassion for him. But forgive? No. There are things in life that should never be forgiven."[3]

To forgive or not to forgive acts of immoral violence—that, certainly, is a complex question.

There is, however, another quality of mercy that is far more straightforward: when it comes to the inevitable disappointments of daily life, parting with blame and grievance will inarguably make us better people. Letting go of the bitterness, the petty grudges, and the festering resentments that populate our lives, and finding it in ourselves to give thanks for our blessings, helps us to change and grow.

Forgive and give thanks. This is the seventh resolution. When we replace grievance with gratitude we move toward the kind of radical acceptance that allows us to find meaning and purpose through life's hardships and limitations. And, here as elsewhere, the solutions we learn with our intimate partners extend into our lives at large, helping us to make growing older a time of surprising possibility.

JAKE AND LEAH LAMBERT

Jake and Leah Lambert seemed the picture of twenty-first-century success. Jake had been a star every step of the way, first at Princeton, then at Harvard Business School, and then at the venture capital firm he had joined after graduation. Leah, likewise, had known little failure. She had excelled at Princeton, where she and Jake had met; at law school; and then at the top law firm where she had quickly become a partner. The couple, now in their late forties, had become something of a fixture in the upper echelons of Boston society: they were friends to the local movers and shakers and were frequent and heavy contributors to charity, and their photographs had graced our newspaper's society columns on several occasions.

Jake and Leah had two children, Stacy, who was seventeen when the couple first came to see me, and Alexander, then fifteen. Stacy was a good kid and a good student, they told me, though lately she had been having some trouble at school. Alexander had had a harder time of it: he had learning disabilities that required him to attend a special school, but, they reassured me, they were getting him the help he needed, and lately he had been doing quite a bit better.

I had the sense that what Jake and Leah told me about the kids barely scratched the surface, particularly in regards to Alexander, but I listened quietly and didn't interrupt; I wanted to focus on why they wanted my help. They certainly needed it: success hadn't prevented Jake and Leah from being deeply unhappy. They fought every evening, often tearing into each other the moment that they came home and removed the plastered-on smiles, the fancy clothes, and the makeup that they had worn to that evening's social engagement. From miscommunications about the babysitter, to disagreements regarding Stacy and Alexander, to Jake's frustration with the lack of sex, their quarrels weren't pretty: words like "asshole" and "bitch" turned up regularly in their arguments.

For the first few weeks I tried to understand how the relationship had become so hurtful. The presence of such unhappiness in the midst of such prosperity wasn't what I found confusing— wealth is no antidote to misery, marital and otherwise—but I was puzzled by the fact that such volatility could grow unchecked between such apparently reasonable and thoughtful people. Outside the relationship neither Jake nor Leah seemed particularly angry or bitter; both had good friendships, and each came across as kind and decent. When the doors to the outside world closed, however, the couple tore each other to shreds.

During our third meeting I noted that Jake and Leah seemed

to be their absolute worst selves with each other, and I asked
whether things had been rocky from the start.

"No," Leah answered, emphatically and immediately. "We
were really happy when we were younger. We met when we
were twenty. We didn't get married until eight years later, but
it wasn't that we had any doubt, there was just a lot of other
stuff we wanted to do. We were even happy together when the
kids were born, so it's not that. The thing with Alexander was
hard, but I feel like we work well together around that. In fact,
that's about the only thing we still do well."

"The thing with Alexander?" I asked.

"Yeah, we told you about that," Leah continued. "He has a
lot of trouble."

"You told me he had some learning disabilities, and that he
was in a special school."

"I guess we were glossing over things a bit," Leah answered.
"He's pretty impaired. Now he's at about a third-grade level in
school, and he's also got a lot of physical problems. He's really
working hard at it, though, and he's getting a whole lot better."

"What's the matter with him?" I asked.

"Didn't we tell you about the accident?" Leah answered.

"The accident?"

"Alexander almost drowned when he was three," Jake said,
now joining the conversation. "We were at our summer place
in New Hampshire, at a Fourth of July party at the lake. Leah
wasn't—I mean, *we* weren't watching; he must have wandered
into the water. We pulled him out, and the lifeguards got him
breathing again, but it took them about twenty minutes. He had
some anoxia, and that affected his brain. He's doing better now,
but it's been slow going. And we've both really worked hard to
help him."

Leah, who was clearly fuming, didn't appear to hear Jake

compliment her on the hard work. I asked her what she was feeling.

"I fucking hate it when you do that, Jake." For the first time the bitterness that the couple had told me about had ignited in my office. "Do you do that on purpose?" she continued, her nostrils flared, her eyes boring into her husband. "That '*Leah* wasn't, I mean *we* weren't watching' bullshit. Fuck you, Jake. We were both watching him. Neither of us was watching him. I wasn't watching him because you were doing what you always do, you were off schmoozing with your useless, soulless investment banker friends. Go fuck yourself, Jake. Go fuck yourself and tell yourself it's my fault."

"Drop it, Leah," Jake answered, biting and dismissive. "I just misspoke. I don't blame you for what happened to Alexander. But you know what I *do* blame you for? For becoming such a bitch over the last ten years."

With this exchange Jake and Leah ushered me into the origins of their troubles. They had endured a tremendous loss, and now they held each other prisoner within a corrosive cycle of blame and recrimination.

ROUNDING UP THE USUAL SUSPECTS

In his book *Western Attitudes Toward Death*,[4, 5] the French historian Philippe Ariès traces the changes that have occurred in our relationship with death. In the Middle Ages, he notes, "death was readily accepted by the living and the dying as a destiny collectively shared." In our modern age, he continues, death has been "banished from life reconceived in terms of short-run earthly satisfactions." We have, Ariès concludes, moved from viewing death as an inevitable, necessary, and even meaningful event,[6] to feeling that it is an unexpected and unwanted intrusion.

Death is an admittedly extreme example of the hardships we

all face (so, for that matter, is a life-altering illness to a child). Nevertheless, the transformation we have witnessed in regard to death is evident in our relationship with all manner of pain. We live in a culture that promises us Teflon-smooth lives lived with a minimum of hardship and a maximum of gratification. We are, it follows, quick to substitute grievance and blame for acceptance when times get tough. "It's not supposed to be this way," we say, when things go badly. "Someone, somewhere must have screwed up."

And whom do we blame? Well, everyone is a possible target, but perhaps the closest and easiest bull's-eye can be found stitched onto the backs of our intimate partners. We are each other's most important persons. We share responsibility for our lives with each other, and we feel an at-times childlike wish to be loved and protected by each other. It is all but embedded in the marrow of our most intimate relationships, therefore, that we will disappoint each other. And so when things go wrong, when it is our impulse to "round up the usual suspects," the names of our husbands and wives are invariably at the top of our lists.

Probably no one can survive the loss of a child without being irrevocably changed. The same is true when a child sustains a dramatic, irreversible injury. The world never again has that same sense of security and possibility, and one's self can never feel quite as whole as it once did.

Hostages to a July evening that had ended in tragedy, Jake and Leah faced a monumental task. If they were to release each other from the bitterness and blame in which they held each other, they would have to help each other to bear what was nearly unbearable. And they would have to do so in a culture that often fails to appreciate the fact that pain and hardship are all part of being a living, breathing human being.

Moving Beyond Blame, but Still Wishing for a Different Past

I began by asking Jake and Leah to do something that I acknowledged would be very difficult: I asked them to talk together about the accident, and I asked them to do so *compassionately*. I organized their efforts by insisting on a single, simple rule: the moment they began to blame they had to separate for fifteen minutes, and during that time they were to remind themselves that what had happened *was* an accident—that was, after all, the word that they had used when they had first told me about it.

The work was tough, but Jake and Leah not only did begin to talk to each other, they took things a step further.

They brought old photographs of Alexander to my office, remembering together the boy that they had known before the accident. For the first time in twelve years they returned to the lake where their son had nearly drowned, and while there they remembered the events of that evening; from the festive party, to the accident, to the hours Alexander spent unconscious, to their joy when he regained consciousness and they realized that he would live, and to their despair when they learned, over the course of several months, that he had suffered life-altering injuries. And they reminded each other of how much they had done to help him; of all the doctors, tutors, and rehabilitative therapists—not to mention the hours of their own time—that they had devoted to his care over the past twelve years.

After several months of hard and painful work Jake and Leah were largely able to accept the notion that what had happened hadn't been either of their faults. Yet though they were able to release each other from blame, all was far from well.

"Until a few months ago we couldn't even talk about Alex without tearing each other's heads off," Leah observed. "So that's better. But I can't say that I feel any better. Every time I see a healthy fifteen-year-old boy I feel, 'That should be Alex.' Every time I see a happy family I think, 'That should be us.' I don't have anyone to pin it on anymore, but I feel just as bitter. What happened to the life we were supposed to have?"

"I have to get over it," Leah continued. "We both do. It's not only a terrible way to feel, it's not fair to Alex. He must feel that we're disappointed in him. That's so unfair, to have something so horrible happen to him and then to have us wish he were different on top of it."

Jake and Leah did need to "get over it," but it was dawning on me that they did not understand just what "getting over it" meant. The couple had stopped blaming each other, and that was good. They had recently been able to cry together when talking about their son, and that was also good. But their tears weren't really tears of acceptance; they were tears of bitterness and grievance, cried for the life that they felt Alexander, and they, *should* have had. And this was not so good.

Jake and Leah needed to make a critical distinction: they needed to get beyond their bitterness and grievance, but that didn't mean that they needed to get beyond their pain and grief.

Trying to clarify, I asked: "What exactly do you mean by 'get over it'?"

"Get beyond all this heartache. Isn't that what you've been telling us?"

"Not exactly," I answered. "You need to get beyond the bitterness, but I doubt that you'll ever get beyond the heartache. I'm reminded of a story. When Ernest Hemingway lived in Paris, friends of his lost two of their children to illness. He wrote them a letter that ended with the line: 'No one you love ever dies.' That line applies in spades to the two of you. Alexander didn't die, thank God, but there is a way that, at least for the two of you, he did die back at that lake. You need to bring him back to life. You need to remember him. You need to get beyond this

'What happened to the life we should have had' stuff. It won't be easy, because remembering him as he really was, and loving him as he really is, is going to be incredibly painful, but if you want to get over your bitterness you have to stop trying to get beyond your pain."

Jake and Leah silently considered what I'd said. Leah was the first to speak: "I think I've assumed that you've been trying to get us to where we're not in pain anymore," she said quietly. "And on some level I think I felt that that just wouldn't be right. I'd feel like I was forgetting Alexander, betraying him. So what you said feels true."

"That does help," Jake joined in. "But this feels like one of those things that seems clear in here when we're talking about it with you, and then when we leave it gets all cloudy. Do you have some kind of trick that would help us to remember what you're saying?"

I had to think for a moment; I'm not usually one for catchy phrasings. Eventually, after an uncomfortable pause, I offered: "How about this? If grievance is the act of wishing for a different past, then mourning is the act of accepting that past in order to allow a different future."

A Priest's Help

Over the next few months Jake and Leah redoubled their efforts: talking, continuing to look at photographs, trying to hold on to the idea that they loved Alexander as he now was. But while they understood the necessity of arriving at a deeper kind of acceptance in their rational minds, achieving that acceptance in their feeling selves was another matter: "I feel like we're doing all the right things," Jake said, "and our relationship is definitely better. But there's not a lot of joy in our lives."

Jake paused for a moment, and when he did speak his words mirrored my own silent thoughts: "Maybe we just need to accept the fact that this is as good as it's going to get."

Then help came from a surprising source: a priest.

Jake and Leah had married in the Catholic Church, but as adults they had done little more than attend the occasional Christmas Mass with the kids. Largely on an "it-can't-hurt-so-why-not-try-it" whim they decided to talk to their parish priest about Alexander. What they got was completely unexpected.

Jake and Leah told the priest about what had happened to their son, and he answered with all of the right and expectable responses. When he acknowledged the depth of their pain his words seemed sincere. He understood that the hardship Alexander faced would never fully disappear, and he thought it likely that Jake and Leah would never be without their agonizing sense of loss. Then, an hour or so into the conversation, just as Jake and Leah were concluding that the talk had been helpful but hardly life-altering, the priest shocked the couple to attention.

"I asked him if there was anything we could do that we weren't already doing," Jake told me. "I didn't expect much, so I wasn't surprised when he started by saying that we were doing all the right things. But then he told us that there was one important thing that we—and you—hadn't thought of. He told us to be thankful."

Jake paused to take a sip of water, and then continued. "At first we thought, 'What kind of holy-roller bullshit is this?' But then he told us what he meant. He told us that every life is precious. That we should be thankful for every day we had with Alexander, that we should be thankful for every magical moment we had before the injury, and for every hard, painful, and equally magical moment we have had since.

"'What if your son had never been born?' he said. 'There are gifts to be found in the lives that you have that are as valuable as those you would have found in the lives you didn't have.' "

"Wow," I said. I, too, was moved by what the priest had said.

"And then he kind of kicked our butts," Leah added. "He said: 'God put you on this earth to take care of this child. He put you here to take care of your daughter too. It's not our place to choose our mission, it's our job to accept the mission that we are given. This is your mission. Be thankful for the opportunity.' "

Through my work I have had the privilege of intimately knowing many people over many, many years. Because individuals and couples sometimes talk with me for long periods, I have had the opportunity to see lives unfold in real time. I have also had this privilege because, even when therapies are shorter, my patients often return, on a few occasions after being away for as many as twenty years. Sometimes they return to work on new problems, sometimes to work on old ones, and sometimes they return just to let me know how their lives have gone. From this rare perspective I've learned that time can often be unkind, but I've also learned that time can be a powerful healer; over the years our remarkable capacities for resilience, perseverance, and creative change unfold, allowing us humans to find solutions where often there seemed to be precious little hope.

Jake and Leah stopped meeting with me regularly within a few months of their conversation with the priest, but for the next ten years they returned once or twice a year, occasionally to talk over thorny issues, more often just to talk. I wouldn't say that they ever achieved the lightness that they had hoped for, and their memories were never free of the pain of Alexander's accident. They did, however, find their way to hopefulness, optimism, and a sense of deep and abiding purpose.

In no small way Alexander's continued recovery helped; by his mid-twenties he was living independently, he attended community college and worked part-time, and he had a girlfriend. But even if Alexander's growth had not continued, I sensed that Jake and Leah would have found their way to more satisfying lives; they had radically altered the way they thought about what they once called "our tragedy."

"The child that we have *is* a gift," Leah told us, many years after we had first begun meeting. "Having children teaches you about yourself, but having an injured or troubled child *really* teaches you about yourself. Jake and I have found capacities in ourselves that we never knew we had."

"Would Alex's life have been better if the accident had never happened?" Leah continued. "Probably, but you just can't think about it that way. Would our lives have been better if the accident had never happened? You know what? I actually don't know the answer to that, which is an amazing thing to say. And I do know this: we are better people than we would have been if everything had gone according to plan."

Leah paused for a moment, smiling a wry smile. Then she added: "According to plan? That's comical, isn't it? You know what else we've learned? There never was a plan. Life just is what it is."

FORGIVING AND GIVING THANKS TOGETHER

We won't find our way to well-lived lives by looking for "right answers"; right answers, such as they are, are all too often temporary, self-serving reductions of life's infinite complexity. A far more powerful path can be found by understanding that we have to make choices, often hard choices, in the face of a never-ending series of paradoxes.

One of the most fundamental of these paradoxes involves the tension that exists between our need to change our lives on the one hand, and the importance of accepting the hand that we have been dealt on the other. Neither choice alone offers a solution: if we believe that everything can be changed we will be forever frustrated and disappointed, whereas if we accept everything that happens as inalterable fate we will be passive and helpless. When considered together as an irresolvable tension, however, these polarities offer us a valuable, if never fully solvable, equation for living.

Radical acceptance, the solution to this life-paradox, involves replacing grievance with gratitude and so finding meaning, not despite life's hardships and limitations, but because of them. This solution, which is captured with the words of the Serenity Prayer,[7] will help us in our efforts to live well, and especially to live well as we grow older, when the necessity to mourn without despairing becomes ever more acute.

Of course we can pursue the resolution to "forgive and give thanks" on our own. The same is true of the other three resolutions described in the latter half of this book (believe in something more important than yourselves; give up your habits and addictions; and play). But, as is also the case with these other three resolutions, forgiveness and gratitude can be deeply and indelibly achieved through our willingness to be vulnerable and real in our long-term, intimate relationships.

Once again, our intimate partners are by and large our most important persons. Because we share responsibility for our lives with them, because they are magnets for our disappointments, it is all but written into our marriage contracts that we will blame them when things go wrong.

But what happens when we make a point of doing the opposite? What happens when we let go of our proclivity to blame and resent our lovers for our own disappointments? Every time we forgive and thank each other we teach each other critical, and generalizable, life lessons: There is no master plan. There is no life that we were *supposed* to lead. There is no good future in wishing for a different past. The assumption that things should always go our way, and that someone or something is to blame if they don't, only leads us away from the path to our better selves.

So what are a few mental Post-its that can help us to remove those bull's-eyes from our partners' backs, and to instead teach each other that signature lesson of growing older: that life derives meaning, and that we derive happiness, by accepting those things we cannot control, by making the most of them, and even, odd as it might sound, by being thankful for them?

- **Find your resentments.** Every relationship has them. Same with hurts and disappointments. Find those too. Acknowledge them, talk about them, and do so without blaming.
- **Don't assume that you are more responsible for what is good in your lives than your partner.** Often both members of a couple feel that they have contributed more, and that their own contribution is underappreciated. Correct for this bias. It is likely more equal than it feels.
- The same goes for what is bad in the relationship. **Be suspicious, very suspicious, whenever you feel that troubles are more your partner's fault than your own.**
- To quote the spiritual writer Henri Nouwen,[8] **remember that "Our sufferings and pains are not simply bothersome interruptions of our lives."** We are who we are, he reminds us, not despite our pain, but because of it.

And if you feel you're on your own?

- For starters, **don't blame and resent if you do have to assume the lion's share of the responsibility.** Indeed, consider it an opportunity for you to grow.
- When you can't engage your partner in a discussion of what

is wrong, **make a point of trying to understand what is your part.** Understand that some part of it is *always* yours.

- **Be willing to acknowledge what is your part without the expectation that your partner will respond in kind.**
- **Be aware of what you have to be thankful for, and be vocal about it.** One of the great hurts that members of a couple tend to feel is that of feeling underappreciated. Give appreciation, and, if need be, give without the expectation of getting appreciation back.
- Once again, **model.** The most powerful way to change your partner is to change yourself.

The Twenty-Year-Old Joke

Lying in bed, in pajamas that he never used to wear, Nick listened to the familiar cycle of nightly sounds: brushing teeth, gargling and spitting, water running in the sink, toilet flushing. He looked up from the book that he was reading, less out of interest than out of a need to finish, toward the bathroom, toward his wife. She was walking purposefully for the bed, but, he could tell, not toward him. He knew that she was angry.

Sophia's straight line from face-washing and toothbrushing to bed and book was meant to leave little room for her husband. She was indeed angry at Nick. He had made that joke again tonight— the one about her being some rare species of plant that couldn't be transplanted outside of New York City. It wasn't funny the first time he told it, and twenty years of telling it hadn't made it any funnier.

He knew that she was angry about the joke. Truth be told, he felt kind of embarrassed about having told it: he knew it wasn't funny, he knew it would make her mad, and he knew that it revealed a place of private unhappiness between them. But he was angry with her too, and probably that was why he told it. It seemed to him that after twenty years of living in Boston she might be able to accept the fact that this was where they had made a pretty good life. It seemed to him that it would be nice to occasionally go out to dinner without having to hear about how the restaurants are better in New York.

"Look, I'm sorry about that old joke. I know it pisses you off. But don't you think just maybe once we could do something together without you making me feel like I'm a minor-league guy who dragged you to a minor-league town?"

"I don't feel like you're a 'minor-league guy,' Nick," Sophia snapped. "Why do you have to personalize everything?" She looked down at him from beside the bed, her crossed arms crushing her breasts into her chest.

Sophia thought back on the move to Boston. Nick had gotten a job offer that was too good to pass up. The timing was terrible. Her mother was dying, and her father—"my schmuck of a father," she still called him—seemed to think that the occasion of his wife's pancreatic cancer was the perfect moment to turn his secretive, ten-year affair into a public relationship. Moving to Boston meant leaving her mother to the nurses, to the hospice workers, and to her self-centered sister, who always took their father's side.

"Why do you still blame me for something that happened twenty years ago, and that you and I *both* agreed to?" Nick asked. "Your mother has become a saint since she died, but as I recall, your relationship with her wasn't all that great when she was alive."

"Let's drop it, Nick. We never get anywhere with this." Sophia's voice was softer, but it wasn't the softness of reaching out, it was the softness of being tired of a twenty-year argument that seemed to do little more than scrape the scabs off old wounds. She got into bed, close enough to her husband to disguise the distance, and she held her book a little further in front of her, a little tighter, than felt natural.

After a few pages she put the book down. "Can I turn out the lights, or are you going to read?"

"You can turn them off," he said, businesslike, with just enough bite that she could feel his unhappiness, but not so much that she would have to call him on it.

"Are you picking up Danny after school tomorrow?" Her tone was also business, but it was business without the irritation. She meant to change the feeling—a silent struggle of the tones.

"Yep, Thursday is my day," he answered, and she could hear that he had yielded. He, too, was tired of the argument.

"Maybe there are just some things you never get through," she said, staring at the ceiling. "Some things you just have to live with."

Nick could hear that kindness had now crept into her voice, alongside the resignation. He felt his shoulders relax, and his throat unclench. "I really am sorry about the joke. As soon as it was out of my mouth I wanted it back."

"I'm sorry too," Sophia said, rolling away from him. Then, reaching back with her foot to touch his shin, she added, "That was such a lousy time back then. Can you believe that I still haven't gotten over it?"

"It was an awful time," Nick answered. "But I understand this not getting over it stuff. Sometimes I think that there are just some things that never stop hurting."

CHAPTER VIII

PLAY

Danielle, a wide-eyed four-year-old girl with long brown hair, walked into my office. She smoothed her yellow sundress, looked warily around the room, and then, squeezing her mother's hand even more tightly than before, began to suck her thumb.

"This is Doctor O'Connell," her mother said.

As I shook Danielle's tiny (and slightly moist) hand, she asked, "Are you the doctor who is helping Mommy with the lump in her breast?"

"No," I answered, "I'm the doctor who helps her with how she feels."

"Good," Danielle answered. "Because her body is making her sad."

Danielle's mother and I sat in our chairs while Danielle wandered around the room. We were meeting in my wife's office; because she is a child psychiatrist her office, unlike mine, has the advantage of being filled with toys, and so I had borrowed it for the occasion. Danielle made her way to the antique doll that sat on the bookshelf, and she held it close to her chest. "Poor baby," she said.

I wondered what was the matter with the doll.

"She doesn't feel good," Danielle answered.

"Oh my," I said. "What's the matter?"

"She needs a doctor." With this Danielle placed the doll gently on the floor and walked purposefully to the desk on the other side of the room. Somehow she had noticed the stethoscope that my wife uses for taking blood-pressure readings, and now she picked it up, walked back to the doll, and continued her examination.

"How do things look?" I asked, following a pause that I hoped was long enough to respect the gravity of her work.

"Everybody is worried about her," Danielle answered, "and she's worried too. But there are good people helping her, so I think she's going to be OK."

Danielle's mother, you've probably gathered, was being treated for breast cancer. Even though the prognosis was good, and even though Danielle's mother and father were doing a terrific job of balancing being reassuring and yet still honest with their kids, fear filled the household.

Danielle, however, was a resourceful little girl, and she did what healthy children do to come to terms with the complexities and pains of life and growing up: she didn't talk things through, she played. She played at being a doctor. She played at being a patient. Not only at this moment in my wife's office, but over and over again, day in and day out, she played, in a way that was at once real and not real,[1] all manner of games related to illness and cure, to dread and hope. Her games brought her fear of her mother's real-life illness into the flexible playground of her imagination, and there, in a universe of fluid rules, she was able to commingle her dread with hope and possibility, thus softening the hard realities that she faced without denying them.

Danielle couldn't change the fact of her mother's illness. But she could, through her play, change her relationship to that illness.

Children have much to teach us. They see the world largely

without guile and agenda (until they learn that there are parts of themselves that they must learn to hide). They speak without fear of telling the truth (until they are taught to do otherwise). And, until they are caused to lose their innocence, they are able to live in their bodies without shame. What's more, they have immediate access to the single most powerful mode of turning unbearable pain into constructive energy: far better than most adults, they know how to play.

Play,[2] this is the eighth resolution.

From Michael and Susan's creation of a new kind of lovemaking in the face of Michael's impotence, to Noah and Devon's bedtime ritual, to Ethan and Olivia's crying game, and to Peter and Stephanie's foundation, creative, intimate play helped these couples find their way back to essential parts of themselves that had been lost to pain. By playing together they became more whole together.

Growing older involves accumulating life experience in a way that allows us to know ourselves, and the world around us, generously, hopefully, and with a minimum of denial. If reality is to bring us meaning rather than despair, however, we need to learn to soften life's hard edges with hope rather than illusion. Which means that we need to learn how to play.

GERRY AND EMMA KELLY

Gerry Kelly was a shade under six feet tall,[3] with tousled gray hair and a body that appeared to have once been quite athletic, but was now noticeably paunchy. With a shy glance he entered my office, and, seemingly unaware of his wife who followed, made his way to a chair. Once seated he glanced up at me and said nervously: "Don't ask me, I just work here."

"Work?" I asked. "Is marriage a job?"

"Job? That sounds pretty awful, doesn't it? It's not a job. But

Emma feels like we need some help, and, hey, what can I say, she's probably right."

"So what do you need help with?" I would soon learn to appreciate Gerry's thoughtfulness, but at this moment I reflexively looked at Emma, assuming that she would be the one to fill me in.

Which she did. "I don't know, exactly. Maybe years of taking each other for granted?" In contrast to Gerry, Emma seemed at ease; in my office, in a body that seemed healthy, if a bit on the thin side, and in loose-fitting clothes that were built more for comfort than for style. "I don't exactly know how to put this. I feel like we are really nice people. That doesn't exactly sound like a bad thing, but I mean we're *pathologically* nice. Like you could do a television show about us, and you could call it the Nicelies. 'And this week the Nicelies almost have an argument,' that would be our show. Great concept, except that it would be so boring nobody would watch it."

"Doesn't your sense of humor help with the boredom?" I asked.

"We are funny. Or maybe I should say we *were* funny. Gerry used to be a riot when he was out with his friends, especially after he'd had a couple of beers, but he doesn't even do that so much anymore. So yeah, we used to be funny. That 'Nicelies' thing was a kind of running joke. But now we're mostly just boring. Nice, but boring."

Gerry and Emma had met and married in their late thirties, and over the past fifteen years their lives had descended into a kind of stultifying stability. Gerry, an engineer, still worked for the company he had joined immediately after graduate school, and while he made reasonable money he would have made a great deal more had he risked going after the stock options and promotions that had been available to him over the years. Emma worked as an epidemiologist at a local medical school, and while she hadn't ascended the ranks academically, her job as a teacher and researcher was secure. Together the couple was financially comfortable, particularly given that they had decided not to have children. "I have some regrets about that," Emma had said. "But neither of us feels like this world is a very safe place to bring kids into. And maybe neither of us feels we'd be very good at making it any safer for them."

"I guess we're a pretty average couple, except for the no kids part," Gerry said. "But we didn't start out that way."

And therein lay two amazing stories.

Gerry went first. He was one of nine kids born to a working-class Boston Irish family; his father had been a union man, an amateur boxer, and a professional drinker His mother, like her husband a devout Irish Catholic, had been a quietly despairing woman; depressed, timid, and overwhelmed by her husband and her many children. By the time Gerry was thirteen he was often truant, he had begun to drink beer and smoke pot, and he even ran some numbers for a local bookie. (Ironically, he counted his father among his customers.)

But then Father O'Malley, a priest from the local parish, be-friended him.

Over the next four years Gerry stopped by the rectory every day after school. He did his homework under the priest's watch-ful eye, and, with O'Malley's encouragement, he left the bad crowd he had been hanging out with. After a while he opened up to the priest, telling him about his home life, his fears, and his privately held hopes and ambitions. Mostly Father O'Malley just listened, and he encouraged Gerry to go to school and do his homework. Sometimes he would buy Gerry lunch, and some-times he and Gerry would wrestle together. "I loved it," Gerry said wistfully. "Every bit of it. Especially the roughhousing. My father never touched me except to hit me. I got my life together because of O'Malley—without him I'd either be on some street corner holding out a cup, in jail, or dead."

Then, midway through Gerry's senior year in high school, shortly after he had received a scholarship to Holy Cross College, Father O'Malley told him that he would be leaving the parish. "He never told me where he was going or why. He, O'Malley— you know I haven't been able to say his name for years—was really matter-of-fact about it. I didn't cry or anything, I just did what I learned to do when I was a kid—I shut down. But underneath I was really upset. A few days later my father told me, in his typically asshole way, 'Hey, I heard they caught that faggot priest of yours groping a kid. Always wondered what you were doing down there after school every day.'

"Later I learned that what my father said was true," Gerry continued, "but it never made sense to me. When I think back, I wonder—was there something wrong with the way he looked at me, talked to me? And then there was the wrestling. I know that I loved it at the time, but now when I think back it feels creepy. But for whatever reason, he never pulled any of that pedophile crap with me."

Gerry paused, and then his eyes welled with tears. "I still wonder, why not me? I know this is sick, but sometimes I feel jealous. But that doesn't make sense to me either. It really felt like he cared about me. So maybe he didn't screw around with me because he *did* care about me. You can hear how fucked-up I still am about this. I just don't get it. I never have."

By the time Gerry finished talking, our first hour had come to an end. Emma and I sat silently, moved by what we had just heard. Probably a full minute passed before she broke the silence: "And that's just the half of it. Next week I'll tell you where I come from."

True to her word, Emma began our next session with her story. "I'm Jewish," she began. "I don't know whether I told you that in our first session, but my maiden name is Rosenbaum. And while I'm not a particularly religious Jew, being Jewish is a really important part of who I am. And, I'm afraid, who I'm not."

Emma's parents' lives had been forged in atrocity. Her father had been a young boy in Minsk at the start of the war, and he had miraculously survived the murders committed by the Einsatzgruppen in 1941 and 1942. He had spent the remainder of the war hidden by neighbors who were members of a small underground, and after the war he found his way to the United States. Emma's mother, meanwhile, had been a young girl living in Holland during the Nazi occupation, and she had also been protected by the underground. A few months before the end of the war, however, she was betrayed, caught, and deported to Terezenstadt. Fortunately her time there was short, and she lived to see the camp liberated. She emigrated to the United States, and there she and Emma's father met and married. Emma and her sister were born shortly thereafter.

"My parents survived the Holocaust—barely. And when you've been through something like what they went through, some craziness is going to get passed along, I don't care how sane you are going in. Lots of times my parents were depressed, they'd cry about their relatives who hadn't made it out, they were terrified that my sister and I would be abducted and killed—they lived with all the stuff that goes with being a survivor.

"But one thing was different about them. Other Jewish kids I knew whose parents were in the camps, or whose parents had relatives who were killed, never talked about it. But my parents spent their entire lives trying to understand how the Nazis could do what they did. My father was even a professor of German studies. And they also tried to make sure that they never acted like Nazis. They were strict vegetarians, during the sixties they protested against the war, they demonstrated against the death penalty, all kinds of nonviolent stuff. They were admirable, terrific people. But they were deeply scarred. They were so terrified of violence that they couldn't even discipline us."

Emma paused, her face reddening. "I remember the one time my father raised his voice to me," she eventually continued. "He thought he was going to have a heart attack. Literally. My mother had to take him to the emergency room, where they told him it wasn't a heart attack but a panic attack. I think that was the last time I ever saw him angry."

As do most children of parents who have endured terrible trauma, Emma had carried forward the burdens of the previous generation. "I remember in medical school I actually fainted the first time we did dog surgery. I thought about the medical experiments at Auschwitz and then I just keeled over. I wanted to be a pediatric surgeon, but I went into epidemiology because I was terrified of doing procedures on my patients. And now here I am, a researcher in public health. It's OK, but like so much in my life it's a compromise."

"Like your marriage," I noted.

"Like my marriage," Emily answered. "I figured Gerry was this tough Irish guy from South Boston who'd run numbers and gotten in fights when he was a kid, who'd pulled himself up by the bootstraps and made a life for himself. I thought he could make me, this terrified Jewish intellectual from Brooklyn, a little less scared. Little did I know he was just as scared as me."

PLAYING WITH TIME

Perhaps you have noticed an interesting twist in the stories I've told thus far: not only do our long-term, intimate relationships help us learn how to live well with the hardships of the present, they also offer us the opportunity to go back in time, and so to heal the pain of the past.

"To go back in time?" You may wonder what kind of backpedaling this is, to suggest that love can override reality's rules and take us back in time. After all, isn't the signature challenge of getting older supposed to be gracefully and optimistically meeting life as it is?

Well, in one of life's more remarkable paradoxes, long-lasting love does allow us to become time-travelers.[4] When we lose ourselves during sex, and in those brief, delightful moments when the light catches our lovers' faces just right and we see them as we remember them from years ago, we momentarily recapture the infatuation of our early months together. This temporal sleight of hand also occurs when we regress into childlike states of need and dependency and we find ourselves living into younger, less grown-up parts of ourselves, as well as when we find our way back to shared memories of precious times gone by. In these and other intimate experiences we bring breath and energy from our younger pasts forward into our aging presents.

The capacity that lovers have to create a degree of fluidity around the usually unyielding edges of time does, of course, also spell trouble: it's no easy thing, for example, when a mild rebuke from an irritated spouse triggers years of humiliation felt at the hands of a critical parent. But this movement through time and emotion also offers a powerful tool:[5] as each of the couples described in this book illustrates, love's time machine allows us to bring parts of ourselves that have been battered and frozen by past injuries into the present day. We can then heal and thaw those parts of ourselves, making us more resilient.

Of course, time itself does not heal all wounds; if on revisiting earlier injuries we merely replay old scripts, we will do little more than reinforce the fears that grew from those injuries.

If we are to rewrite old scripts, if we are to let go of the self-protective but self-limiting habits, beliefs, and solutions that block our paths to change and growth, we have to recognize and celebrate the ways in which our lovers, and our present-day relationships, differ from our past experiences. And then we have to learn from those differences.

This is where play[6] comes in, the kind of play to which Aristotle referred when he wrote: "Play that you may be serious."

So what, exactly, is play?

Well, for starters, play is a natural reparative inclination that lives in all of us. As the little girl Danielle demonstrates, we see this inclination most strongly in children, but it is equally present in adults; it just tends to be hidden behind convention, embarrassment, fear, and other forces that limit our spontaneity and authenticity.

And how does play occur?

We don't schedule play,[7] and we don't consciously agree to play. We don't negotiate beforehand the rules and scripts of our play. Play happens largely on its own terms, and our only real control lies in whether or not we allow it to unfold. But by following the resolutions described in this book, by being open, by being real and vulnerable with each other, we can allow our naturally reparative inclination for play to emerge.

And finally, what does play do?

When it occurs in an intensely private and safe intimate space, play allows us to bring elements of our previously non-negotiable pasts into creative collision with each other. In ways that are at once real and not real, that simultaneously embody both past and present, and that allow for the immutability of history alongside the possibility of change, play enlivens parts of ourselves that have become deadened, lightens parts that have become too heavy to carry, and teaches us how to live with pains that have all too often become too great to bear.

Gerry and Emma would never be able to change the historical realities of their painful pasts. But if they could learn to play together, they might be able to reengage old injuries together in the present, and so help each other to become a little less scared, and maybe even a little less "nice."

Playing (and Wrestling) Their Way to Freedom

I encouraged Gerry and Emma to take a few risks. I asked them to talk more to each other, to be a little more angry when called for, to express a little more desire when they felt it. Basically, I asked them to be a little less "nice." Emma would never betray Gerry in the way that Father O'Malley, and his own parents, had, I argued. And Gerry was no Nazi; his aggression would never approach that which Emma had sensed lurking in the shadows of her parents' pasts.

Gerry and Emma bought into what I was saying, but their will to change was undermined by their many safety-ensuring habits. Gerry overate, Emma exercised a bit obsessively, and at the top of the list was television. "Bad television," as Gerry put it. "We like all the cheesy shows. *The Bachelor, The Amazing Race, Survivor*; you name it and we watch it. Basically we just drug ourselves with bad television and then we go to bed."

It wasn't hard to get Gerry to go for a little less food, and Emma a little less exercise. The television, however, was another matter. Eventually I proposed a rule: one show a night, to be jointly selected.

"Kicking the habit," Gerry noted. "Are you going to prescribe the methadone?"

Over the next few months Gerry and Emma did manage to stick with our one-show-per-night resolution, but they struggled with how to fill the newly opened space. More snacks for Gerry and more exercise for Emma were the obvious choices, but the couple resisted the temptation to substitute one habit for another, and gradually they began to turn to each other. This was the desired outcome, but again, it wasn't easy.

"The other night, after *Survivor* ended, we looked at each other with this 'OK, so what do we do now?' kind of look," Emma began. "It was really, really awkward. There we were, we'd been married twenty years and we didn't even know what to say to each other when we turned off the tube."

"What did you end up doing?" I asked.

"It was a beautiful evening, and Gerry suggested a walk. I even took his arm. A group of teenagers walked by. They seemed like nice kids, talking and joking, a little crazy but not too crazy, if you know what I mean. Gerry asked me if I had any regrets about not having children. Can you believe that? *My husband, Gerry Kelly,* asked me what I was feeling. So I told him that yeah, I did regret it. I wish I could do it over."

"And you?" I asked Gerry.

"I have lots of regrets these days," Gerry answered. "And not having kids is the biggest one. I didn't believe I could be a good father. I still don't, but I wish I'd tried."

Gerry's hands were clasped so tightly in front of his forehead that the muscles in his forearms strained, and, instead of looking at Emma or me he seemed to be staring at the patterns in my rug.

"You look unhappy," I noted, stating the obvious.

"I know that things are getting better between us," Gerry answered, his voice barely audible, "but sometimes I wake up in the middle of the night with this horrible thought. Do you know who Raoul Wallenberg was? I know about him through Emma's family. He was a Swedish diplomat stationed in Budapest during World War II. When the war ended the Russians jailed him because they thought he was an American spy. They probably executed him soon after the war, but for years there were rumors that he'd been sighted in one or another Soviet work camp."

"Anyway, I always wondered how he would have felt if he'd

actually lived, and if he'd been freed thirty, forty years later," Gerry continued. "Would he have wanted the little bit of life he had left? Could he have stood the pain of knowing how much life he had lost?"

Gerry paused, then, looking up from the rug for the first time since he had begun speaking, asked, "Are we going to get enough out of this to make up for having wasted all those years?"

Now it was Emma's and my turn to stare at the rug. After several uneasy moments she broke the silence: "My parents were really screwed-up people because of what happened to them. But maybe also because of what happened, they had some wisdom. My father used to say, 'Just do the right thing. Things don't always work out, but if you make decisions that you can live with you'll be OK.'"

"I'm not bailing out, Emma," Gerry answered, speaking with surprising conviction. "I'm just talking about how I feel." Then, looking at his wife with a wry smile, he added, "But I'll tell you one thing. A little more fun would help to ease the pain. And a little more sex wouldn't exactly hurt either."

Emma, too, found herself yearning for more physicality in their relationship. Unfortunately sex was, as Emma put it, "one big, hairy mess" for both her and her husband. Whenever Gerry approached Emma sexually he thought about O'Malley, and, as he pointed out in his humorously dark way, "Thinking about how the priest you loved almost fucked you, and then on some level feeling hurt that he didn't, that's not exactly a turn-on." Emma, too, found that sexual desire sent her hurtling back into the confusions of her inherited past: "You can't really want anything in that deep-down, in-the-body way if you can't let yourself feel forceful," she said. "Lately I feel more like making love, but it isn't easy for me when my model of forcefulness is the

Nazis that almost killed my parents while they were murdering six million other Jews."

Gerry and Emma needed to bring those parts of themselves that had become contorted by old fear and pain into real and present-day contact with each other. They needed to teach each other that vulnerability and desire could lead to something other than betrayal and murder. Sex would be a terrific way to rewrite these old scripts, but their sexual relationship was tangled up in the very issues that they most needed to change.

Then they got some help from an old friend: bad television.

Nearly a year after we had begun working together, Gerry and Emma entered my office wearing broad smiles. After trading shy glances and what I thought might even have been stifled giggles, Emma began:

"So the other night we were watching *The Amazing Race*. One of our favorite couples—and I hope by now you know us well enough to know that when I say 'favorite couples' I'm being tongue-in-cheek—was even more nasty than usual. It actually looked like the guy was going to start slapping his girlfriend around right there on national television. So I said to Gerry, mostly joking, 'Why can't we fight like that?' And before I knew it we were rolling around on the living-room floor wrestling."

Emma noticed the surprise on my face. "Do you have to notify the authorities?" she asked teasingly.

"It depends," I teased back. "Are either of you in danger?"

"Depends what you mean by 'danger,'" Gerry answered. "We ended up making love. You don't have to report that, do you?"

Gerry and Emma's wrestling became a frequent ritual, one that ushered in an entirely new kind of sexual relationship. Sometimes they just wrestled. Sometimes their "horsing around," as they came to call it, led to sex. And sometimes they made love without the wrestling. Whatever the mix, their playful, safe physicality was the epitome of deep play: a creative way of transforming the constraining pain of their respective pasts into something new and healing. And through it Gerry found his way back to a sense of vitality that he had lost since O'Malley had betrayed him, while Emma found a safe way to express forcefulness that had previously seemed so dangerous and scary to her.

Toward the end of one of our final sessions, now nearly two years after we had begun, Gerry and Emma paused the conversation unexpectedly, looking sheepishly at each other. Emma spoke first:

"Maybe before we stop we should tell him about that thing we never told him."

"Sure," Gerry said. It seemed clear from his response that he even relished the idea.

"We didn't really mean to hold out on you," Emma said. "But maybe we both felt a little weird about it, and when neither of us brought it up during the session right after it happened, we both just let it go."

"So what happened already?" I asked, playfully impatient.

Emma took a sip from her coffee, pointedly making me wait a bit longer. Then she continued. "OK, so one night we were doing our Ultimate Fighting Championship thing—everything in life has a television reference, you know—and Gerry was pinning my arms to the floor. I was getting a little turned on. But he was also holding me tighter than usual, and it was starting to hurt. All of a sudden I got furious. I screamed 'let go,' and when he did I slapped his face as hard as I could."

Emma's face reddened, perhaps from embarrassment, perhaps from the powerful emotions that her story had triggered. After another sip of coffee—perhaps this time it was more like a gulp—she continued: "I was really scared for a second, and I think Gerry was as stunned as I was. But then we looked at each other and we both started to laugh. I thought about my father going to the emergency room that time when he got mad at us, and it made me laugh even harder. Not at my father, it's terrible that he was so scared, more like I was laughing because I felt free. Less 'nice,' less stuffed up inside myself. Free."

MARITAL WORK, MARITAL PLAY

In her book *Against Love: A Polemic,* sociologist Laura Kipnis[8] offers up a witty indictment of modern love and marriage. Among other notions, she argues:

⬦ That the work required to make a relationship last drags us into a sinkhole of soul-stifling drudgery.

⬦ That everything that follows those heady, early stages of desire compromises our freedom and self-expression.

⬦ That fidelity involves sacrificing one's sexuality and desire for the complacent safety of domesticity.

At first glance Kipnis's treatise seems seductively radical, an invitation—a challenge, really—to reject the staid institution of marriage for an alternative lifestyle that allows a more full expression of one's self. But is her argument correct? For that matter, is it even radical?

For starters, there is no doubt that relationships do take work. Self-reflection, acceptance of responsibility, open and honest talk, respect, and avoidance of blame, denigration, and rationalization—all these and more take hard work. But since when is this kind of work demeaning to the human spirit? Sticking with our commitments even in the face of conflict, loss, and vulnerability need not be self-stifling drudgery, it can be the work of a well-lived life.

Now let's take things a step further.

In today's society, a society in which self-interest and self-involvement have become the convention, trading in mutual commitment for individual gratification is hardly a radical notion. These days, it follows, taking the risk of allowing ourselves to be changed through a long-term commitment is the *real* radical choice.

But none of this change can happen without play.

When we engage each other in real and playful ways, we touch those places that have been most injured, and are therefore most closed to growth, with love, kindness, and compassion. We bring our deepest fears into creative contact with each other. In ways that are at once real and not real, that simultaneously embody both past and present, play, once again, invites seemingly immutable aspects of our histories into the present, and so enlivens parts of ourselves that have become deadened, lightens parts that have become too heavy to carry, and teaches us to live with pains that have all too often become too great to bear.

Without play, all that hard work would be just that—hard work. Our relationships might be better, but they would reach but a fraction of their potential.

When, however, good relationship work serves as a base layer, and when we add to that base layer the catalyzing, transformative presence of play, then sustained intimacy can become a high-risk and high-reward exercise in change and growth. And staying together, ironically enough, becomes the *real radical choice.*

So what are some specific guidelines that can help us to radicalize our marriages, and help us to play in ways that allow us to be changed by each other?

- **Set the bar high.** Don't just ask your relationship to be better, ask it to change you.

- **Let go of convention, embarrassment, and self-consciousness.** These stifle playfulness. Try to remember what it felt like to be a child, and how free you may have felt to play back then.
- **Find that playful self that may have become lost in your marriage.** Has the humor gone out of your relationship? Try to remember what you once found funny together. Don't take yourself too seriously.
- **Institute games and rituals.** Play sometimes needs a framework, and it can emerge spontaneously once it has one.
- **Talk about your craziest, and most painful, interactions.** Focus on the most repetitive. Then find the themes. More than likely, there is a repeating script in these interactions that reflects a core dilemma for each of you. Don't judge each other for these scripts; remember, we're all screwed up in one way or another. Instead find some lightness and humor.
- **Don't wish for a different past.** Play together in a way that can change your relationships to that past.

And for those of you trying to get your partner to come out and play:

- **Remember that we don't schedule play.** We don't negotiate the rules beforehand. Play happens largely on its own terms, and our only real control lies in whether or not we allow it to unfold. Put your effort into making room for your partner to play.
- **Find light ways of teasing your partner.**
- **Search out your partner's embarrassment and shame, and try to counter it.** Remind him or her that we are all screwed up. ("It's really OK—we're all human.")
- Finally, **poke fun at yourself.** Again, **model.**

Life chips away at so much of what we once took for granted. It is our job, as we get older, not to feel that time is taking everything away. Playing together can make this job a great deal more fun.

"Be Nice, Xena"

"You're the boss, Christina."

She had been giving him the list of things she needed for the night's dinner party—flowers, food, wine—and she had been doing it in that competent, "Let's get it done, and let's get it done without the bullshit" way she had. Usually that way was OK with him, but this morning he'd woken up feeling lousy, and when he felt lousy her hardness didn't roll off him quite so easily. And so his "You're the boss, Christina" had more than a little irritation to it.

Christina hadn't missed that irritation. "Give me a break, Justin. Just do it," she'd answered, meeting his anger and then raising it.

"Breathe," she thought, mostly mocking herself. (All this mindfulness stuff still felt pretty corny to her.) But breathe as she might, she couldn't dissolve the anger in her belly. She hated it when her competence irritated him, even more when it made him act like a little boy. His little boyness took her back to the five-foot-three-inch, one-hundred-and-ten-pound behemoth of a girl that she had felt like when she was fifteen. That was when her father's depression had hit full force, and she had taken care of him and her overmatched mother by growing up in a hurry, making sure that her childish needs didn't add to the family's burdens.

She looked at her hands. They were the one part of her body that still seemed small when she felt too big. Looking at her hands helped her more than the breathing.

He wasn't sure how to answer her "just do it." He knew that it was a bad idea to speak from feeling hurt: he still remembered how stung he had been when he complained that she referred to their two children as "her" kids rather than "theirs," and she told him that she might feel differently if she didn't have *three* children to care for. Buying time, he looked for a pen and a piece of paper.

"Tell it to me again, I'll make a list." He was careful to keep his feelings out of his voice.

Like his wife, Justin's trouble keeping himself in scale dated back to when *his* father's life had fallen apart. There had been a series of business failures, and his mother had taken over the house, creating the illusion of order. "Don't bother your father, he's working," had been his mother's refrain. "Working," they all knew, meant that their father was locked in his office, obsessively reading the financial pages, bemoaning his misfortune, and whining about all the "idiot bastards" he knew who had gotten ahead of him. But it wasn't the loss of his father that had left him feeling like such a helpless little boy; he never had much of the man to begin with. It was the loss of his mother, who had traded in her kindness for an angry competence.

"Butter, fish—whatever looks good—lemon, maybe some salad. I want to keep it simple." Christina was also buying time. She could tell that Justin was trying, and that knowledge did what her breathing couldn't do—it softened her anger. Which gave her a way out of the quarrel.

"Thanks so much for doing the shopping, honey," she cooed, with special emphasis on the "honey." "I know that you're a busy and important man."

Those same words, delivered with even the slightest hint of derision, would have infuriated him. But her tone was all play. So was her devilish smile. Even her reference to his importance felt a little serious. "One pill makes you larger"; her teasing worked like a potion, returning him to his adult size. From this place of feeling better he was able to find his line.

"Be nice, Xena."

Xena—there was a blast from the past. Back before the kids were born, back when they had enjoyed the unimaginable indulgence of sitting at home on Friday nights with nothing to do, watching *Xena: Warrior Princess* had been a favorite pastime. The show had spawned a joking routine, one that had given them a way out of this zero-sum game of size that seemed to sometimes take over their relationship. It had given Justin a foothold in distinguishing between Christina's solidity and his mother's cold, angry competence. And it had given Christina a way to feel strong without feeling too big (the warrior princess was, after all, a princess too, and what was more, as they often remarked, she had quite a wardrobe).

"And flowers, too," Christina added, pointedly ignoring Justin's reference, though they both knew it had helped. "Not those huge stalks you usually get, the ones that make it so we can't see each other across the table. Something a little more delicate."

BECOMING WHOLE TOGETHER:
"I AM BECAUSE WE ARE"

Josh and Maria Rhigetti settled into their chairs and glanced uncomfortably at each other, and then at me. "So where do we start?" Maria asked.

"Wherever feels most important," I answered.

After an uneasy pause, Josh, a heavyset man in his mid-forties, dressed in an expensive suit that was too rumpled to be stylish, began. "How about the fact that we bring out the absolute worst in each other?" Josh spoke with an irritated intensity, and I couldn't tell whether he meant to talk constructively about a problem that he wished to solve, or whether he merely wished to blame Maria for the fact that he felt so lousy.

Maria, a trim, stylishly dressed woman whose thinness seemed more strained than healthy, thought she knew what Josh meant. "He sounds reasonable," she said, clearly angry. "Like he's talking about something we both need to work on. But what he really means is that I'm impossible, and he's stuck with me."

"Christ, Maria," Josh answered, his anger now rising above that of his wife. "I can't say anything without you acting like I'm beating you up."

"Poor Saint Josh," Maria answered scornfully. "Having to put up with his pathetic bitch of a wife..."

"Is this what happens between you guys?" I interrupted. I was a bit taken aback by how quickly things had ignited, and my voice reflected my surprise.

"Sorry," Maria answered, clearly embarrassed. "This is what happens when we try to talk about our relationship. What Josh said about 'bringing out the worst in each other' is true. We *aren't* like this with anyone else. Does that mean that maybe we shouldn't be together?"

PARTS IN SEARCH OF A WHOLE[1]

Often in the early stages of work with a couple, I have heard the words: "I'm not like this with anyone else." I have learned to be skeptical of these proclamations. Or perhaps I should say that I have learned to be skeptical about what these proclamations imply: that one has been driven by one's partner to act in a way that is completely foreign to one's own self. Sure, our worst selves often do come out with those we love, but it is rarely true that the responsibility is solely theirs. Marriages bring out our best selves, they bring out our worst selves, and they bring out all parts of our selves, including and especially those we have long buried.

In this way long-term intimacy allows us a rare view into a surprising aspect of our human natures: we are less continuous than we imagine ourselves to be. In a sense our selves are like motion pictures; they are composed of multiple freeze-frames that we stitch together with our minds, making ourselves feel more unified than we really are. Generally this underlying multiplicity feels seamless, though the fissures in our selves that result from pain and trauma can be profound.

The Polish poet Wislawa Szymborska eloquently describes what can happen when we are under extreme duress:

In danger the holothurian cuts itself in two.
it abandons one self to a hungry world
and with the other self it flees.

from Szymborska's "Autonomy"[2, 3]

As it is for the holothurian, such dividing (the clinical term for which is "dissociation") is initially adaptive for us humans. But it also has its downside. At its worst, our capacity for dissociation allows us to do terrible things to one another. Consider racism and sexism. In this present-day version of witch-burning we disavow aspects of ourselves that we fear, we banish those aspects into others who are different from us, and we denigrate and attack those others, often justifying our actions in the service of God, nationality, and other familiar vehicles for our self-righteousness.

And of course, far more benign examples of dissociation can be found in everyday life. How often do we do things and say things that we can't believe we did or said? (Was that my evil twin?) And how many of our arguments, our unjustified criticisms, and our failures of tolerance, kindness, and decency can be traced to our difficulty accepting painful aspects of our own selves?

The stories that fill these pages are replete with examples of how embracing our whole selves can enable us to live better lives.

When Michael Smithson reconnected with the insecurity he felt as a youth, he was able to stop putting Susan down, and when Susan opened herself to the anger and disappointment she felt at her father she was able to know Michael more accurately.

When Noah Rosenbaum remembered and mourned his mother, he no longer compared Devon to an impossibly idealized version of femininity, and when Devon reconnected with feeling betrayed by her father she began to trust Noah.

By embracing their working-class backgrounds, Peter and

Stephanie Silva found the motivation to change the lives of underprivileged teenagers.

And by opening themselves to their traumatic pasts, Gerry and Emma Kelly found the playfulness that they needed to live more fully.

These couples did something that we can all benefit from doing: by building bridges between different elements of their consciousnesses, by connecting to parts of themselves that had been bruised and fearful, they knit together fuller and more solid selves.

Establishing a more fluid and open discourse between disparate aspects of our experience is a lifelong endeavor, one that may never be fully achieved. But it is one that is well worth the effort. By being open to all aspects of ourselves, we can be honest about our hatred and our intolerance, we can be open about the fears and vulnerabilities that cause these feelings, and we can use this honesty and openness to hold ourselves to a higher moral standard. We can, in sum, bring all of ourselves to bear on life's many challenges.

Josh had grown up with an abusive father and, in an effort to be different, he had committed himself to kindness. Cruel was the last thing he imagined that he was with Maria—if anything he saw himself as something of a long-suffering victim. But despite his best efforts Josh *was* his father's son, and his sadism emerged in his marriage.

Josh wasn't alone. While Maria also thought of herself as the victim in the relationship, she, too, could be cruel. Her father, who had favored her two brothers, had belittled her, even to the point of paying their private college tuitions while insisting that Maria attend a state school. As is so often the case, her anger at her husband took the same form as her father's. She denigrated and demeaned Josh, making him feel insignificant in the same way that her father had her.

Josh and Maria really were not, as they put it, "like this with anyone else," and as a result they were terribly upset to realize how injurious they could be to each other (it is extremely disquieting to realize that one is not exactly who one imagines oneself to be; even more so to realize that one can be precisely what one has spent one's entire life trying not to be). But accepting these disturbing aspects of themselves, even accepting that they goaded each other in an effort to draw out each other's worst selves, proved powerfully transforming. Ultimately Josh and Maria's willingness to own their disavowed anger and cruelty allowed them to govern themselves more thoughtfully, and so to bring kindness and respect back into their marriage.

"I hated myself for how I was being," Maria said, some eighteen months after we had begun our work. "Not that Josh wasn't playing his part—he was, and it's helped me a lot that he's been willing to admit that—but underneath, who I really couldn't stand was me. It was a vicious cycle. I would treat him badly, I'd hate myself for how I was being, the more I'd hate myself the more I'd blame him, and the more I'd blame him the more I'd hate myself.

"It's strange," Maria continued, becoming quite pensive. "Sometimes there are things about ourselves that we absolutely can't admit, as if it would be the worst thing in the world if they were true. And then when we finally do admit them, it turns out to be a relief. Sort of like 'OK, I can stop trying to fool everybody. I can even stop trying to fool myself. I guess I'm just a regular old human being after all.'"

EIGHT INTIMATE RISKS
AND ONE RADICAL ANSWER

My work with Josh and Maria helped them to make their relationship better. Their relationship, in turn, made them better. Herein lies the ultimate take-home message of this book. When it comes to marriage:

✧ We are each other's most important persons.

✧ We accompany each other through the relentless passage of time.

✧ We tend to know each other more intimately than we know anyone else, and tend to be known as well in turn.

And so our long-term intimate relationships can:

✧ Shake us out of our familiar comfort zones.

✧ Teach us to accept, and learn from, realities that we cannot control.

✧ Help us to grow into our fullest, most complete selves.

The eight resolutions outlined in these pages are meant to guide us.

The first four, "shared necessities," lay the foundation for keeping our relationships vital and alive through the many conflicts, many hardships, and many changes of long-lasting intimacy:

• **Embrace a longer-lasting vision of love.** When we learn to love each other across all of the seasons of our lives, we learn that time can be *con*structive as well as *de*structive, and

that growing older can bring us increasing, rather than diminishing, possibilities.

- **Celebrate your differences.** When we learn to appreciate
each other as beings in our own right, rather than experience each other as extensions of our own wishes and needs,
we open ourselves to the kind of new experience that keeps
us vital and growing, even as we grow older.
- **Have real sex.** When we learn the value of living in our
bodies over time, we repudiate the Teflon-smooth, virtual sexuality that surrounds us, and we instead appreciate the visceral and more enduring rewards of authentic
physicality.
- **Find liberation through commitment.** When we are willing to tie ourselves in, lean back, and let go with each other
over many years, we find the kind of freedom that comes
from knowing and accepting our whole selves.

These first four resolutions help us to create safe, shared
spaces in which we can risk being real and vulnerable with
each other in minds, selves, and bodies. In the process, they
also teach us critical life lessons, lessons that are in many
ways organized around the central tenet of midlife wisdom:
we don't find purpose and meaning *despite* the realities that
delimit our lives, we find purpose and meaning *because of
them.*

The second four resolutions ("shared choices") go beyond
the goal of building and sustaining a long-term relationship,
emphasizing the way that shared, intimate risk-taking can cata-
lyze personal growth:

- **Believe in something more important than yourselves.**
When we believe in things that are more important than
ourselves we learn humility; we value persons, principles,

and ideas in their own right, and so allow life itself to really matter.

- **Give up your habits and addictions.** When we rid ourselves of our self-limiting and self-protective behaviors, we force ourselves out of our familiar safety zones, and we expose ourselves to the kind of new experience that leads to change and growth.
- **Forgive and give thanks.** When we give up the belief that we are entitled to perfect and painless lives, we appreciate our fallibility, and with this our deeper humanity.
- **Play.** When we bring long-lost parts of ourselves into new and transformative contact with our present-day partners, we take an important step on the never-ending journey of making ourselves more whole.

These latter four resolutions provide us with a creative, organizing framework in which we can encourage, even challenge, each other to live into our best, and most whole, selves.

Taken together, these eight resolutions offer us an emphatically positive, and these days radical, answer to the question "why stay together?" Because the key to living fully and creatively as we get older is continued growth, and the most growth-promoting possibilities imaginable can be found in the unexplored depths of our long-term intimate relationships.

UBUNTU:[4] "I AM BECAUSE WE ARE"

At the heart of these eight resolutions, and of the overarching premise that our intimate relationships can help us to grow into our best selves, lies a fundamental human principle: we are not beings unto ourselves, rather we are who we are by way of our relationships. This principle is captured by a wonderful South

African word—ubuntu." Loosely translated, ubuntu means "I am because we are."

It's no surprise that we have to look beyond traditional Western language to find a word for this deep sense of human interconnectedness. While Eastern culture has long emphasized our place in the larger order of things, Western culture, relatively speaking, emphasizes the individual. This is not a recent phenomenon. As Daniel Robinson of Georgetown University notes, the ancient Greeks were the first people who actually considered "their deepest convictions, their deepest sentiments, as subjects for critical appraisal and study." Robinson cites the famous inscription at the temple at Delphi: "Know thyself."[5]

Unfortunately, our once-positive willingness to reflect upon our selves has now morphed into a problematic "me-first" mindset. Unfortunate because narcissistic cultures such as ours are characterized by a problematic paradox: the more that there is a single-minded emphasis on the individual, the less likely it is that individuals living in that culture will have healthy, solid selves.

But here is where our long-term relationships offer us a powerful antidote.

Ubuntu—"I am because we are."

Because long-term intimacy causes us to find parts of ourselves that have been long hidden, our relationships serve as forums in which our authenticity and fallibility can be appreciated rather than denied.

Because we continue to love and touch each other as we grow older, our relationships allow us to remain emotionally and physically alive even as our bodies age, and as our losses, compromises, and disappointments accrue.

And because when we change and grow we cause each other to change and grow, our relationships help us to achieve the renegotiation of self that is necessary if we are to live our lives with grace, purpose, and authenticity.

When all is said and done, the message of this book is really quite simple: Merely making our relationships last is just not good enough. Our relationships can change us. Our relationships should change us. Our relationships will change us for the better—if we are willing to take the risk.

The Call Home

"Are you getting enough sleep? Are you getting your work done?"

Zack could tell from his wife's words and voice that she was talking to their son. Eliza was never that concerned when their daughter called. Cheryl never needed much reminding or prodding, but Sam, who now was bigger than any of them, and who had spent last summer navigating his way through Europe with a backpack, still elicited Eliza's motherly worry.

After a few minutes Eliza handed the phone to her husband. Zack loved hearing Sam's voice; he was still amazed by how deep it had become, and by the thoughtfulness and perspective that had blossomed in the young man over the past few years. But the conversation never seemed to flow quite as easily as it did with Eliza. This evening Sam had called them, and on those rare occasions when this happened (they almost always had to call him if they wanted to talk to him) there tended to be an ever-so-slight sense that the young man wanted something that he couldn't quite say. His mother seemed to find it easier to negotiate this landscape of vague and uncertain need, while Zack found himself saying, "I don't want to keep you" much sooner than he really meant.

"Our boy seems pretty good," Eliza said, as she watched Zack slowly place the phone back in its cradle.

Zack noticed the "our." When the children were little, Eliza often referred to them as "my" kids. She always denied that it meant anything, just "a quirk of phrasing," she would say, but

Zack knew that it was more than that. Years later, when they learned to be more honest about things, she told him that they did sometimes feel more like her kids than their kids. After all, she was the one who knew about their friends, their appointments, their worries. Zack didn't love them less, he was just less involved with the stuff of their everyday lives. And so, even now, when they needed something, he felt a touch of that old feeling of being on the outside looking in.

"He seems really good. But I worry he's working too hard."

Eliza smiled. Things had changed a lot since the days when Zack, who was working way too hard himself, used to complain that the kids didn't know the value of hard work. Back then her job had been to get him to ease up on them, to reassure him that they were just kids, and that they were going to be OK.

The call now over, Zack and Eliza looked at each other tentatively. For twenty years their shared sense of purpose had made the next conversation easy to find; there was always the next school meeting, the next kid to drive, the next game to attend. But now that both kids were off at college—first Cheryl and now Sam—the house felt different. Not exactly an "empty nest," more disorienting than empty. They had to find their way back to just the two of them again, back to the beginning, and yet it couldn't quite be the beginning. That wasn't bad, it was even kind of exciting, but it wasn't easy.

"What do you feel like doing this weekend?" Zack asked. Where once the ritual was "What do we *have to do* this weekend?" now it was "What do you *feel like doing?*"

"There's a movie playing at the Coolidge I wanted to see. One of those foreign films, you know, about relationships and stuff. Not really up your alley, but at least it has some sex in it."

Zack smiled at the old joke. "Hey, I'm into relationships these days," he said. "Especially relationships with sex."

Later that night, after they had found their way to bed, Eliza rolled over onto Zack's chest. She missed the way he used to feel—his muscles were softer now—but there was something comfortable about the softness. His body felt more like hers, and she found it easier to fold herself into him. It also helped that these days she could lie on him without him always immediately wanting to make love.

Zack was thinking about the phone call with Sam. His son sounded great. He could sense Eliza in Sam—he admired his wife's directness, even if it did annoy him when she trained it on him, and Sam seemed to be developing that same "no bullshit" clarity. But he was also a bit of a romantic, like his dad, and while that hadn't played so well with the girls in high school, where edgy cool seemed to be today's ultimate trump card, it seemed, from the hints that Sam had been dropping, that it was playing better in college. And then, of course, Sam was becoming his own man. Not Eliza, not Zack, not even a combination of the two. More a bunch of parts that had become their own surprising whole.

Like their relationship. Fifteen years ago they had fought over the direction their lives would take. From how to raise the kids, to where to live, to where to go for dinner, they were two selves strug gling over what shape they would carve from the single stone of their togetherness. But then, somehow, the struggle had ended, and the stone had found its own shape. And so they lay in bed, a little sad, a little scared and also a little eager, gazing together into the surprisingly uncertain future.

◯*√*OTES

INTRODUCTION: GROWING UP TOGETHER: MIDLIFE CHALLENGES AND MIDLIFE RELATIONSHIPS

1. Rhonda Byrne, *The Secret* (New York: Atria Books, 2006).

2. Steve Pavlina, "Intention" (http://www.stevepavlina.com/blog/2005/10/cause-effect-vs-intention-manifestation/. Pavlina writes: "After I declare my intention, I wait for the resources and synchronicities to arrive. Usually they begin to manifest in 24–48 hours, sometimes sooner."

Chapter I. Embrace a Longer-lasting Vision of Love

1. Jeffrey Eugenides, *Middlesex: A Novel* (New York: Picador, 2003).

2. Helen Fischer, *Why We Love: The Nature and Chemistry of Romantic Love* (New York: Henry Holt, 2004).

3. J. N. Edwards and A. Booth, "Sexuality, Marriage, and Well-Being: The Middle Years," in *Sexuality Across the Life Course,* edited by A. S. Rossi (Chicago: University of Chicago Press, 1994).

4. Paul Ehrlich writes: "Genes and environments are fundamentally connected, and they interact in complex ways—something we must always keep in mind when we necessarily, but artificially, separate them for purposes of analysis and discussion." Paul Ehrlich, *Human Natures: Genes, Culture and the Human Prospect* (New York: Penguin Putnam, 2002).

5. S. Van Goozen, V. M. Wiegant, E. Endert, F. A. Helmond, and N. E. Van de Poll, "Psychoendocrinological assessment of the menstrual cycle: The relationship between hormones, sexuality, and mood," *Archives of Sexual Behavior* 26, no. 4 (1997): 359–382.

6. D. Marazziti and D. Canale, "Hormonal changes when falling in love," *Psychoneuroendocrinology* 29 (2004): 931–936.

7. M. Beauregard, J. Levesque, and P. Bourgouin, "Neural correlates of conscious self-regulation and emotion," *Journal of Neuroscience* 21, no. 18 (2001): RC165.

8. Helen Fischer contrasts the MRI studies of subjects in love done by her group with: B. A. Arnow, J. E. Desmond, L. L. Banner, G. H. Glover, A. Solomon, M. L. Polan, T. F. Lue, and S. W. Atlas. "Brain activation and sexual arousal in healthy, heterosexual males," *Brain* 125 (2002): 1014–1023.

9. From Helen Fischer, *Why We Love.*

10. D. Marazziti, H. S. Akiskal, A. Rossi, and G. B. Cassano, "Alteration of the platelet serotonin transporter in romantic love," *Psychological Medicine* 29 (1999): 741–745. Also, Laurie Barclay, "Love is all in your head—or is it in your genes?" *WebMD Medical News*, February 14, 2001.

11. A. Bartels and S. Zeki, "The neural basis of romantic love," *NeuroReport* 2, no. 17 (2000): 12–15; and T. Esch and G. Stefano, "The Neurobiology of Love," *Neuroendocrinology Letters* 26, no. 3 (2005).

12. Esch and Stefano write: "regions commonly activated in love, as known so far, are strongly involved in reward physiology, comparable to an acute administration of euphoria-inducing drugs, such as cocaine." T. Esch and G. Stefano, "The Neurobiology of Love."

13. Fortunately this vision may be more of a caricature than a truth. Perhaps one reason for the strength of this caricature is that most theories are based on couples in therapy, not naturalistic studies of couples. Indeed, in one such naturalistic study, Boston psychologist Stuart Andrews found that the accepted paradigm of romantic love followed by painful disillusionment was far less prevalent than most of us imagine.

14. As biologist Sue Carter puts it, "Love can be defined as a group of processes, experiences, and behaviors that promote and maintain social ties." C. Sue Carter, "Bonding, Benevolence and Health," in *The Science of Altruism and Health*, edited by Stephen G. Post (London: Oxford University Press, 2006).

15. Bartels, A. and S. Zeki, 2000, "The neural basis of romantic love." From Helen Fischer, *Why We Love*.

16. The brains of subjects in the Bartels and Zeki study "showed heightened activity in the caudate nucleus and the ventral tegmental area, two of the brain's primary reward centers." From Helen Fischer, *Why We Love*.

17. Data on testosterone in this paragraph taken from: James McBride Dabbs, *Heroes, Rogues and Lovers: Testosterone and Human Behavior* (New York: McGraw-Hill, 2000); A. Booth and J. M. Dabbs, "Testosterone and men's marriages," *Social Forces* 72, no. 2 (1993): 463–477; and S. J. Berg and K. E. Wynne-Edwards, "Changes in testosterone, cortisol, and estradiol levels in men becoming fathers," *Mayo Clinic Proceedings* 76, no. 6 (2001): 586–592.

18. Our understanding of the role of oxytocin and vasopressin begins in an unlikely place—research on a small midwestern American rodent called the prairie vole. Prairie voles are interesting to us because in contrast to some 97 percent of mammals, prairie voles are monogamous. Thomas Insel and Larry Young, neuroscientists from Emory University, found that immediately upon mating, prairie voles, in contrast to their nonmonogamous close cousins the montane voles, release oxytocin and vasopressin (oxytocin in females, vasopressin in males) into their brains. These chemicals generate a pleasurable sense of well-being, and this sense of well-being in turn creates a positive association with the vole's recent sexual partner. Monogamy made easy! T. Insel and L. J. Young, "The neurobiology of attachment," *Nature Reviews Neuroscience* 2 (2001): 129–136, and T. R. Insel, Z. Wang, and C. Ferris, "Patterns of brain vasopressin receptor distribution associated with social organization in microtine rodents," *Behavioral Neuroscience* 14 (1994): 5381–5392.

19. This, along with dopamine and norepinephrine, which appear to be related to attraction, spells out Helen Fischer's heuristically useful tripartite system for love over time: sexual desire, attraction, and attachment.

20. Louis Cozolino notes that interactions between mothers and young infants lead to a "biochemical cascade" of oxytocin, prolactin, endorphins, and

dopamine. These neurochemicals stimulate the maturation of the brain, the growing of neural networks, and they cause pleasurable feelings, leading to the wish for further contact. Louis Cozolino, *The Neuroscience of Psychotherapy: Building and Rebuilding the Human Brain* (New York: W. W. Norton, 2002).

21. P. Zak, "Trust: A temporary human attachment facilitated by oxytocin," *Behavioral and Brain Sciences* 28, no. 3 (2005): 368–369.

22. Esch and Stefano refer to the relationship between attachment and the release of oxytocin and vasopressin after intercourse. T. Esch and G. Stefano, "The Neurobiology of Love."

23. As Susan Carter of the University of Chicago puts it, "Oxytocin is a hormone associated with emotional safety and security. It down-regulates stress hormones and encourages positive social behavior. This in turn feeds back and opens the way for more sociality." From C. Mims, "Addicted to Love," *ZooGoer* 33, no. 3 (2004).

24. Recent research suggests that Jon Bowlby was right: attachment is itself a primary human need. The long-held Freudian view—that attachment is a secondary phenomenon that results from our need to satiate our primary instincts of sex, hunger, and so on—is largely inaccurate. Biologically speaking, longer-term attachment is as important a piece of the puzzle of love as is sexual drive. Of course this makes sense. After all, while we have to mate to survive, we also have to raise our young, and as human beings, with infants helpless and needing care so much longer in life than other mammals, the endurance of a parental bond also proves essential to our survival.

25. Prostate cancer statistics from Montefiore Medical Center, 2005.

26. Robert Solomon, *About Love* (Lanham, MD: Madison Books, 2001).

CHAPTER II. CELEBRATE YOUR DIFFERENCES

1. Stephen Mitchell, *Can Love Last? The Fate of Romance Over Time* (New York: W. W. Norton, 2002).

2. Eric Kandel, *In Search of Memory: The Emergence of a New Science of Mind* (New York: W. W. Norton, 2006).

3. Mark Solms notes that Kandel demonstrated that there is a two-stage process related to memory. Initially "short-term memory appears to involve reverberating circuits—groups of interconnected cells firing together in closed (self-rejuvenating) loops. Initially, the cell changes are purely physiological, in that the synapses connecting the cells in the circuit become more 'permeable.' This, in turn, sets off a second, more permanent, anatomical process. The continual firing of cells at certain junctions activates in the cells genetic mechanisms that promote the growth of further synapses at those junctions." Mark Solms and Oliver Turnbull, *The Brain and the Inner World: An Introduction to the Neuroscience of Subjective Experience* (New York: Other Press, 2002).

4. From Louis Cozolino, *The Neuroscience of Psychotherapy: Building and Rebuilding the Human Brain* (New York: W. W. Norton, 2002); Joseph LeDoux, *The Synaptic Self: How Our Brains Become Who We Are* (New York: Penguin Books, 2002); Mark Solms and Oliver Turnbull, *The Brain and the Inner World: An Introduction to the Neuroscience of Subjective Experience* (New York: Other Press, 2002); and Susan Vaughan, *The Talking Cure: Why Traditional Talking Therapy Offers a Better Chance for Long-Term Relief Than Any Drug* (New York: Henry Holt, 1997).

5. As scientist and author Thomas Lewis puts it, "At a Lilliputian level, the brain is an elaborate transducer that changes a stream of incoming sensation into silently evolving neural structures." Thomas Lewis, Fari Amini, and Richard Lannon, *A General Theory of Love* (New York: Random House, 2000).

6. Joseph LeDoux, *The Emotional Brain* (London: Weidenfeld & Nicolson, 1996; New York: Other Press, 2002).

7. Salman Rushdie, *In Good Faith* (New York: Penguin, 1990).

8. Thomas Lewis, Fari Amini, and Richard Lannon, *A General Theory of Love.*

9. Susan Vaughan writes: "Intensive psychotherapy works . . . by allowing our encoded patterns to come to life in full force through the relationship with our therapists. The reawakening and re-experiencing of the core patterns gives us a chance to really work on our prototypes of self and other, questioning their hidden assumptions about reality one by one, and in the process defanging them." Susan Vaughan, *The Talking Cure: Why Traditional Talking Therapy Offers a Better Chance for Long-Term Relief Than Any Drug.*

10. One final thought in regard to married minds and changing brains: Until recently theories of learning relied heavily on the notion that our brains are most amenable to change and growth when we are young. There is now a great deal of evidence that this assumption is flawed. Maturing brains are far more "plastic" than was previously understood, and have tremendous capacities for learning and change. We can, it follows, continue to reshape the core dilemmas with which we have long struggled throughout our lives, even, and in some ways especially, as we grow older.

Chapter III. Have Real Sex

1. Parts of this paragraph and the next from Mark O'Connell, *The Good Father: On Men, Masculinity and Life in the Family* (New York: Scribner, 2005).

2. From Mark O'Connell, "The Epidemic of Meaningless Teenage Sex," *Boston Globe*, March 9, 2005.

3. Joyce McDougall, *A Plea for a Measure of Abnormality* (New York: International Universities Press, 1980).

4. Robert Stoller, *Porn: Myths for the Twentieth Century* (New Haven: Yale University Press, 1991).

5. From M. Parsons, "Sexuality and perversion a hundred years on," *International Journal of Psychoanalysis* 81 (2000): 37–52; J. Whitebook, *Perversion and Utopia* (Cambridge, MA: MIT Press, 1995); and J. Chasseguet-Smirgell, *Creativity and Perversion* (London: Routledge, 1985).

6. Psychoanalyst Jim Herzog has proposed a tentative scheme for the varieties of psychological meaning found in male intercourse in his book *Father Hunger*. Men, Herzog notes, engage in destinative intercourse ("I am a man, I can do it"), recreative-interactive intercourse (which stresses the "hedonic and social aspects of the act"), procreative intercourse (which is aimed at making a baby), parentogenic intercourse (which couples the wish to make a baby with the intent to care for it), and integrative intercourse (which results in a feeling of oneness and wholeness with one's partner). From James Herzog, *Father Hunger* (Hillsdale, N.J.: Analytic Press, 2002).

7. From Mark O'Connell, *The Good Father: On Men, Masculinity and Life in the Family*.

CHAPTER IV. FIND FREEDOM THROUGH COMMITMENT

1. Of course living well doesn't involve passive acceptance, it involves accepting that which cannot be changed, and endeavoring to change that which can and needs to be changed.

2. American psychoanalyst Otto Kernberg writes: "A preconsciously adhered to set of values is gradually mapped out, elaborated and modified through the years, and provides a boundary function for the couple vis-à-vis the rest of the world." Otto Kernberg, *Love Relations: Normality and Pathology* (New Haven: Yale University Press, 1995).

3. This paragraph is taken from a large body of literature, including: D. W. Winnicott, "Mirror Role of Mother and Family in Child Development," in *Playing and Reality* (Harmondsworth, England: Penguin Books, 1967/1980); T. B. Brazelton, E. Tronick, L. Adamson, A. Als, and S. Wise, "Early Mother-Infant Reciprocity," in "Parent-Infant Interaction," *CIBA Foundation*, Symposium 33 (Amsterdam: Elsevier, 1975); J. Herzog, "Early Interaction and Representation: The Role of the Father in Early and Later Triangles and Triads" (Stuttgart: Schottaur, 1998: 162–179); and James Herzog, *Father Hunger*; D. Stern, *The Interpersonal World of the Infant* (New York: Basic Books, 1985); K. Clarke-Stewart, "The Father's Contribution to Children's Cognitive and Social Development In Early Childhood," in *Father-Infant Relationship: Observational Studies in a Family Setting*, edited by F. A. Pedersen (New York: Holt, Rinehart & Winston, 1980); R. Corwyn and R. Bradley, "Determinants of Paternal and Maternal Investment in Children," *Infant Mental Health Journal* 20 (1999): 238–256; D. Ehrensaft, *Parenting Together: Men and Women Sharing the Care of Children* (New York: Free Press, 1987); M. Lamb, "Mothers, Fathers and Child Care in a Changing World," in *Frontiers of Infant Psychiatry, Vol. II*, edited by J. Call, E. Galenson, and R. Tyson (New York: Basic Books, 1984); and M. Yogman, "The Father's Role with Preterm and Fullterm Infants," in *Frontiers of Infant Psychiatry, Vol. II*, edited by J. Call, E. Galenson, and R. Tyson (New York: Basic Books, 1984).

4. S. Bem, "The Measurement of Psychological Androgyny," *Journal of Consulting and Clinical Psychology* 42 (1974): 155–162.

5. A useful analogy can be found in the matter of height. Men are, on the whole, taller than women. That does not, however, mean that all men are taller than all women, or that there aren't tall women and short men. We've lost track of this simple truth because ever since Eve was made from Adam's

rib, we have thought of gender as a zero-sum game: if a woman has something then a man doesn't, and vice versa. This win-lose, either-or mind-set affects everything from our understanding of intelligence, where slight differences in standardized test scores lead us to conclude that a woman can't be the next Einstein (a conclusion as absurd as the suggestion that a man could never be the next Virginia Woolf), to political campaigns, where voters are forced to choose between the caricatures of conservative cowboy or liberal wimp.

6. J. Raphael Leff, *Psychological Processes of Childbearing* (London: Chapman and Hall, 1991); and A. Samuels, "From Sexual Misconduct to Social Justice," *Psychoanalytic Dialogues* 6 (1996): 295–322.

7. One final thought regarding the mutual renegotiation of masculinity and femininity in an intimate relationship: Interestingly, though we think of the kind of flexibility noted above as relatively more due to the nurture side of the nature-nurture continuum, it is one that is found in the biology of our maleness and femaleness. Consider the changes that take place across our life spans in testosterone and estrogen levels. As men age their levels of testosterone drop. Meanwhile, as women age their levels of testosterone effectively rise. (Functionally speaking, women's testosterone levels rise not only when testosterone itself increases, but also when levels of estrogen drop. Thus, as women age, and as their estrogen levels fall, their levels of testosterone effectively rise.) Thus relationships tend to move from a biologically based imbalance in sexuality and aggression (more for men than for women early on) toward a more equal distribution of sexual desire and aggression. This rearrangement may be helpful in fostering the kind of compromise and shared decision-making that help relationships to last.

8. Quote from Holly Brubach, *Vanity Fair*, April 2005.

9. C. S. Carter, A. C. DeVries, and L. L. Getz, "Physiological Substrates of Mammalian Monogamy: The Prairie Vole Model," *Neuroscience and Behavioral Reviews* 19, no. 2 (1995): 303–314; C. S. Carter, A. C. DeVries, S. E. Taymans, R. L. Roberts, J. R. Williams, and L. L. Getz, "Peptides, Steroids, and Pair Bonding," in *The Integrative Neurobiology of Affiliation,* edited by C. S. Carter, I. I. Lederhendler, and B. Kirkpatrick (*Annals of the New York Academy of Science,* 807: 260–272. New York: New York Academy of Sciences, 1997); and L. J. Pitkow, C. A. Sharer, X. Ren, T. R. Insel, E. F. Terwilliger, and L. J. Young, "Facilitation of Affiliation and Pair-Bond Formation by

Vasopressin Receptor Gene Transfer into the Ventral Forebrain of a Monogamous Vole," *Journal of Neuroscience* 21, no. 18 (2001): 7392–7396.

10. From Tom Smith, "American Sexual Behavior: Trends, Socio-Demographic Differences, and Risk Behavior," National Opinion Research Center, University of Chicago. GSS Topical Report No. 25. Updated December 1998.

11. Peggy Vaughan, *The Monogamy Myth: A Personal Handbook for Dealing with Affairs* (New York: Newmarket Press, 2003).

12. Holly Brubach, *Vanity Fair*, April 2005.

13. Thanks to: Stephen Mitchell, *Relational Concepts in Psychoanalysis* (Cambridge, MA: Harvard University Press, 1988).

14. Adam Phillips, *Darwin's Worms: On Life Stories and Death Stories* (New York: Basic Books, 2001).

15. Some argue that repeatedly falling in love would be like *Groundhog Day:* we would always come up against the same conflicts and limitations. This isn't exactly correct. To some degree we would "be the same with anybody" (as embittered lovers often say to each other as a way of deflecting blame), but different lovers would also bring out different aspects of our conflicts, different parts of ourselves. In relationships with different people we are, it follows, both the same and different.

CHAPTER V. BELIEVE IN SOMETHING MORE IMPORTANT THAN YOURSELVES

1. Thanks to Ned Hallowell, *Connect: 12 Vital Ties That Open Your Heart, Lengthen Your Life, and Deepen Your Soul* (New York: Pocket Books, 2001).

2. Tom Brokaw, *The Greatest Generation* (New York: Random House, 2001).

3. Thanks to: Philippe Ariès, *Western Attitudes Toward Death* (Baltimore: Johns Hopkins University Press, 1974). (Quoted by Patrick Hutton in Patrick Hutton, "Of Death and Destiny: The Ariès–Vovelle Debate About the History of Mourning," in *Symbolic Loss: The Ambiguity of Mourning and Memory at*

Century's End, edited by P. Homans (Charlottesville and London: University Press of Virginia, 2000).

4. Heinz Kohut, *The Restoration of the Self* (New York: International Universities Press, 1977).

5. Erik Erikson, *Identity and the Life Cycle* (New York: W. W. Norton, 1994).

CHAPTER VI. GIVE UP YOUR HABITS AND ADDICTIONS

1. From, among others, Paul Chance, *Learning and Behavior* (5th edition) (Toronto: Thomson-Wadsworth, 2003).

2. Daniel Gilbert, a leader in the burgeoning field of happiness research, notes that we human beings are surprisingly bad at making ourselves feel good. We make the same errors again and again because we tend to overestimate the pleasure that certain rewards, usually fleeting, will bring. Daniel Gilbert, *Stumbling on Happiness* (Toronto: Knopf, 2006).

3. More modern models of psychoanalysis focus more on the mutative power of a mutual relationship than on the interpretive power of a supposedly objective psychoanalyst.

4. Originally spoken by Marlon Brando in *On the Waterfront,* and adopted by psychoanalyst Steven Cooper as a motto for our modern-day culture of greed and grievance.

5. Kohut lecture.

CHAPTER VII. FORGIVE AND GIVE THANKS

1. Thanks to Edward Hallowell, *Dare to Forgive* (Deerfield Beach, FL: Health Communications Inc., 2004).

2. Wendy Kaminer, *I'm Dysfunctional, You're Dysfunctional: The Recovery Movement and Other Self-Help Fashions* (New York: Vintage Books, 1992).

3. Some who write about the importance of forgiveness argue that the intention of forgiveness is not to forgive the actual crime, rather it is to free

oneself from hatred. Robert Enright and Joanna North, *Exploring Forgiveness* (Madison: University of Wisconsin Press, 1998).

4. This paragraph from Mark O'Connell, *The Good Father: On Men, Masculinity and Life in the Family* (New York: Scribner, 2005).

5. Thanks to Philippe Ariès, *Western Attitudes Toward Death* (Baltimore: Johns Hopkins University Press, 1974). Quoted by Patrick Hutton in Patrick Hutton, "Of Death and Destiny: The Ariès–Vovelle Debate About the History of Mourning," in *Symbolic Loss: The Ambiguity of Mourning and Memory at Century's End,* edited by P. Homans (Charlottesville and London: University Press of Virginia, 2000).

6. Microbiologist Ursula Goodenough writes in her book *The Sacred Depths of Nature:* "Sex without death gets you single celled algae and fungi... Death is the price paid to have trees and clams and birds and grasshoppers, and death is the price paid to have human consciousness, to be aware of all that shimmering awareness and all that love." Ursula Goodenough, *The Sacred Depths of Nature* (New York and Oxford: Oxford University Press, 2000).

7. "Lord grant me the strength to change the things I can, the ability to accept the things I can't, and the wisdom to know the difference between the two."

8. Henri Nouwen, *Life of the Beloved* (New York: Crossroad Publishing Company, 1992).

CHAPTER VIII. PLAY

1. British psychoanalyst Michael Parsons writes: "Play depends on a particular area of the imagination where things can be real and not real at the same time." Michael Parsons, *The Dove That Returns, the Dove That Vanishes: Paradox and Creativity in Psychoanalysis* (London and Philadelphia: Routledge, 2000).

2. "Play." Thanks to, among others, Gregory Bateson, *A Theory of Play and Fantasy, Steps to an Ecology of Mind* (New York: Chandler, 1972); Steven Cooper, *Objects of Hope: Essays on the Limited Possible* (Hillsdale, N.J.: Analytic Press, 2000); Clifford Geertz, *The Interpretation of Cultures* (New York: Basic Books, 1973); James Herzog, *Father Hunger* (Hillsdale, N.J.: Analytic Press, 2002); Stephen Mitchell, *Influence and Autonomy in Psychoanalysis* (Hillsdale,

N.J.: Analytic Press, 1997); Michael Parsons, *The Dove That Returns, the Dove That Vanishes* (London: Routledge, 2000); Adam Phillips, *On Kissing, Tickling, and Being Bored* (Cambridge, MA.: Harvard University Press, 1993); and D. W. Winnicott, "Mirror Role of Mother and Family in Child Development," in *Playing and Reality* (Harmondsworth, England: Penguin Books, 1967/1980).

3. Aspects of Gerry and Emma's story first appeared in: J. Herzog and M. O'Connell, "Children Are Being Murdered: How Do People Live and Play in the Aftermath of Atrocity?" Published in *Children, War and Persecution: Rebuilding Hope* (Proceedings of the Conference on the Effects of War and Persecution on Children at Moputo, Mozambique, December 1st through 4th, 1996).

4. Here as elsewhere, biology offers a useful window into one of our most seemingly poetic phenomena. While systems of sexual desire, attraction, and attachment appear somewhat sequentially, with the former two dominating in the early months of falling in love and the last presiding in the years that follow, these systems are also competing and complementary. The fact that we've turned eighty doesn't keep our testosterone levels from rising in response to a tender kiss, and it doesn't keep dopamine from infusing our caudate nuclei when we take our lover's hand on a moonlit night. And so it follows that even in the unsentimental world of chemistry and physiology there is room for a little romance.

5. American psychoanalyst Otto Kernberg notes that intimate relationships are that rare occasion in which time "does not only act destructively." Kernberg goes on to note that intimate relationships allow the "repair of old conflicts in the crucible of shared intimacy." Otto Kernberg, *Love Relations: Normality and Pathology* (New Haven: Yale University Press, 1995).

6. Clifford Geertz, who described how cockfighting among the Balinese served to express aggression in a way that promoted and preserved, rather than disrupted, social order, provides a conceptual foundation for this idea with his notion of "deep play." Clifford Geertz, *The Interpretation of Cultures* (New York: Basic Books, 1973).

7. Michael Parsons, *The Dove That Returns, the Dove That Vanishes: Paradox and Creativity in Psychoanalysis.*

8. Laura Kipnis, *Against Love: A Polemic* (New York: Pantheon Books, 2003).

CONCLUSION: BECOMING WHOLE TOGETHER: "I AM BECAUSE WE ARE"

1. Many theorists and clinicians have advanced our understanding of dissociation and the multiplicity of self. I am particularly indebted to Philip Bromberg and Richard Schwartz. Philip Bromberg, *Awakening the Dreamer* (Mahwah, N.J.: Analytic Press, 2006); Richard Schwartz, *Internal Family Systems Therapy* (New York: Guilford Press, New Edition, 1997).

2. Wislawa Szymborska, *View with a Grain of Sand: Selected Poems* (New York: Harvest Books, 1995).

3. Thanks to Philip Bromberg for making me aware of Szymborska's poem, and for his contributions to our understanding of dissociation and the multiplicity of selves. Philip Bromberg, *Awakening the Dreamer*.

4. "Ubuntu": Thanks to psychologist Lizzie McEnany for making me aware of this word.

5. Dr. Robinson notes: "With ancient Greece, we get the first evidence of a thoroughly self-critical perspective on one's own basic knowledge claims. We find in the ancient Greek world, and in the ancient Greek world of thought, the first evidence of a people actually recognizing their deepest convictions, their deepest sentiments, as subjects for critical appraisal and study." Dr. Robinson cites by way of example the famous inscription at the temple at Delphi, the temple dedicated to Apollo: "Know thyself." Daniel Robinson, Georgetown University, audiotape.

Acknowledgments

Above all, I wish to thank Karen Murgolo and Paul Bresnick.

Karen Murgolo, my editor, gave me the opportunity to say something that I have long wished to say. For this alone I am hugely grateful. She also taught me, through her gentle and persistent tutelage, to become better at one of writing's most critical tasks: that of achieving clarity and accessibility without sacrificing thoughtfulness.

Paul Bresnick, my agent, has given me one of the greatest gifts one person can give another: an opportunity to be heard. Without his intelligence, persistence, decency, and wisdom, I suspect that I would never have published one book, much less two. And so I would never have had one of the greatest satisfactions of my middle age.

I am also deeply indebted to Jamie Raab, the publisher of Grand Central Publishing; Emi Battalia, the associate publisher of Grand Central Publishing; Tom Hardej, editorial assistant; Diane Luger, art director; Matthew Ballast, executive director of publicity; and Melissa Bullock, also in publicity. The team that has put together this book has been, from beginning to end, an absolute joy to work with.

Finally, this is a book about how marital partners can change each other for the better. But it is also a book that is based on a far more sweeping belief—that we are changed through *all* of our intimate relationships, marital and otherwise. We are who we are as a result of all of our meaningful relationships, both past and present. I have had the good fortune to have been made by many wonderful people; through my work, through my friendships, and most of all, through my family. I am indebted to all of them.

About the Author

Mark O'Connell is a clinical instructor of psychology at Harvard Medical School and Cambridge Hospital. He has twenty-five years of experience working with individuals and couples. The author of *The Good Father*, he has appeared regularly as a guest expert on the Fox News New England network and on NPR and other radio programs. O'Connell lives with his wife and three children in Chestnut Hill, Massachusetts.